RESPONSES TO
LESSONS LEARNED EARLY

Jerry Jenkins's bright, homey anecdotes in *Lessons Learned Early* are like a warm Kentucky quilt.
> Sandy Aldrich
> Associate Editor
> *Christian Herald*

All of these little glimpses into the formation of character are thought-provoking and serve to highlight appreciation for life values that really matter. Many outstanding insights and character-revealing episodes are found in this fascinating collection. Well done!
> Gleason L. Archer
> Trinity Evangelical Divinity School

Jerry Jenkins sees things most of us miss, helps us ponder their meaning, and sends us away refreshed.
> V. Gilbert Beers
> Author

Here Jerry opens up his honest, growing faith and prods us to keep pace.
> Stephen and Janet Bly
> Authors

A masterful storyteller who gently teaches what he has learned so well.
> Dale Hanson Bourke
> Senior Editor
> *Today's Christian Woman*

Jerry Jenkins writes with a hearty combination of humor, biblical insight, spiritual sensitivity, and down-to-earth understanding of human nature.

> Harold O. J. Brown
> Trinity Evangelical Divinity School

Jerry's lessons are delivered with style, charm, and a characteristically hefty punchline!

> Tim Dowley
> Author, Editor

Jerry Jenkins has the God-given ability to take the simple, mundane things of life and present beautiful, rock-solid truths for deep contemplation.

> E. Brandt Gustavson
> Executive Director
> National Religious Broadcasters

I have always been challenged by Jerry Jenkins's ability to say what I wish I had.

> James A. Gwinn
> President
> Christa Ministries

This book clearly shows his astounding ability to bring a reader directly into experiences filled with interest and wit, humor and intimacy.

> Gary Hill
> Annotator
> *The Discovery Bible*

"The world is crowded with God," C. S. Lewis said. "All ground is holy and every bush, if we could perceive it, is a burning bush." Jerry Jenkins has allowed us into his life, to be part of his stories. They are indeed crowded by God. Tears came as I read of the Angela who helped her more talented friends experience church. Mildred's story made me angry—first at the Christian leaders who didn't feel her pain, and then at myself for missing the Mildreds God puts in my life. Joy, grief, laughter: This collection is easy to read, very difficult to forget. More importantly, what God said to me through some of the stories will be impossible not to act upon.

Marlene LeFever
David C. Cook Co.

Jerry has the ability to take the ordinary events of life and show us that they are extraordinary.

Erwin Lutzer
Pastor, Moody Memorial Church

Down-to-earth, practical, to the point, and always with that little nudge to the reader to answer an unspoken question about his/her relationship to Christ. Valuable material to be read around any Christian family's table.

Craig Massey
Author, Speaker

When *Moody Monthly* arrives, the first article we turn to is "For Starters." It is always delightful, well written, and often touches our hearts.

Larry and Diane Mayfield
Composers

Give Jerry Jenkins two minutes—the time it takes to read one of these vignettes—and he will give you a world of insight, fresh thinking, and spiritual perspective. Not many authors can consistently pack this much value into a small space.

Dean Merrill
Vice President of Publications
Focus on the Family

The warmth, humor, and sincerity of Jerry Jenkins fill the pages of *Lessons Learned Early*. I found myself smiling one minute and fighting back tears the next. It is a delightful taste of family life at its finest and Christian principles presented at their most practical level of everyday life. At once convicting and encouraging. I love it!

Lois Mowday Rabey
Author

Warm stories, apt challenges, thoughtful insights.

> Harold Myra
> President
> Christianity Today, Inc.

With a deft hand, Jerry Jenkins does for the page what Norman Rockwell did for the canvas—paints colorful, wry, wistful portraits of people caught in the act of being utterly, captivatingly human. From homespun homilies to barbed bits of arrow-sharp humor, *Lessons Learned Early* is etched with a rare transparency, a seasoned scrutiny, and a style that ensures the author an enduring niche in the reader's heart.

> Carole Gift Page
> Author

Jerry Jenkins is a good story teller. He is warm and he has a sense of humor. He knows how to put his arm around the reader's shoulder and give him truth to hold on to.

> Roger C. Palms
> Editor
> *Decision* magazine

Some writers succeed with style, others with content. Jerry Jenkins succeeds with both and adds a dash of delightful humor as well.

> Norm Rohher
> President
> Christian Writers Guild

It's hard to believe how quickly Jerry Jenkins can slip up on you and get you thinking.

> Doug Ross
> Executive Director
> Evangelical Christian Publishers
> Association

Jerry Jenkins's clear perception of life and its challenges provides a window through which the light of truth floods our souls. His words measure and mold the reader gently, yet firmly.

Joseph Stowell III
President
Moody Bible Institute

Jerry Jenkins reads easy. Blessed with keen perception and refreshing humor, he edifies as well as entertains. These essays probe, penetrate, puncture, but most of all, please. He's one of my favorite people, as well as writers.

George Sweeting
Chancellor
Moody Bible Institute

This is Jerry Jenkins at his best. His humor and insight will cause you to laugh, cry, or say, "I identify with that!"

Sammy Tippit
Evangelist, Author

This collection is outstanding, and we are so pleased to see Jerry's great columns in one volume.

Pat and Jill Williams
Authors
Rekindled

Here is a heartwarming glimpse into the personal life of a fine writer and a remarkable man.

Sherwood Eliot Wirt
Editor Emeritus
Decision magazine

A genuine wordsmith showers us with the delights of polished prose. Be forewarned. This will be a hard book to put down because wit and wisdom so grace its pages in abundance.

John Woodbridge
Trinity Evangelical Divinity School

How refreshing to meet one whose faith is alive and contagious. Jerry skillfully takes Scripture out of the abstract and plugs it into the cutting edge of life. His applications encourage me . . . for I see that God is very much alive and at work in the big and the small of our lives.

Christine Wyrtzen
Recording Artist

Jerry Jenkins is a marvelous writer and a first-rate storyteller. As the Garrison Keillor of evangelicalism, he stirs the mind and warms the heart. With the strength of focused conviction, he communicates with excellence.

Don Wyrtzen
Musician

LESSONS
LEARNED EARLY

JERRY B.
JENKINS

MOODY PRESS
CHICAGO

The articles in this book were originally published
as columns in *Moody Monthly* magazine.

Illustrations by Joe Ragont

ISBN: 0-8024-4687-6

1 2 3 4 5 6 Printing/LC/Year 94 93 92 91 90

Printed in the United States of America

*To Barbara Goodwin
in loving memory of
Jill Wilson
1949–1989*

AMONG OTHER BOOKS BY JERRY B. JENKINS

Nonfiction
   Hedges: Loving Your Marriage Enough to Protect It
   Hymns for Personal Devotions
   Baby Mayfield: Living with the Choice
   Rekindled: How to Keep the Warmth in Marriage

Biographies
   Sammy Tippit
   Hank Aaron
   Dick Motta
   Pat Williams
   Paul Anderson
   Madeline Manning
   B. J. Thomas
   Walter Payton
   Luis Palau
   Meadowlark Lemon
   George Sweeting
   Christine Wyrtzen
   Deanna McClary
   Orel Hershiser

Fiction
   The Margo Mysteries
   The Jennifer Grey Mysteries
   The Bradford Family Adventures
   Dallas O'Neil and the Baker Street Sports Club
   The Dallas O'Neil Mysteries
   The Operative

CONTENTS

FOREWORD

No one can read *Lessons Learned Early* and be unchanged. It's great reading for a busy person who wants to be busier for God and to feel right about what's wrong with the world.

Jerry Jenkins introduces us to people and presents them to be loved, understood, and accepted. And yet somehow, the people to whom he introduces us are people we've known all along at different times and in different settings. It's just that we didn't know that he knew them by other names and in other places, and so much better than we could ever hope to know them.

Few devotional writers speak to the will and make us want to act. The beauty of the short essays in this book is that each of them is like a Norman Rockwell painting. We see, we hear, and we smell almost everything with him. But most of all, we understand, we feel, we want to act.

MOISHE ROSEN
Executive Director
Jews for Jesus

PREFACE
Thanks, Eric

I wrote a column in *Moody Monthly* magazine for years before I finally learned, from my temporary successor, how to do it.

In 1981 I left the magazine for a couple of years, and Eric Fellman became the director. He took over the column then called "Background" (it's now called "For Starters").

I had used the column to simply point out interesting, behind-the-scenes stuff about the articles in each issue. No one ever talked about the column, and I frequently debated its value.

In my last column before moving to other responsibilities, I made brief mention that I would be working on the same floor in the same building, but that I would be turning right instead of left when I got off the elevator.

I was stunned by the response. Several people mentioned that seemingly innocuous line, and even a year later someone asked me if I was still turning right off the elevator.

I didn't give that much thought until I was trying to counsel Eric on the writing of the column. He wrote a little about what was in the magazine, but he began to drift into personal stories about his wife and kids and even his dog.

"Eric," I said kindly, "are you sure people care?"

"Do they ever!" he said. "I'm getting lots of mail."

Mail? That column never got mail! He showed me some of it. Readers loved the personal touch. Eric didn't brag, didn't editorially drag out the family slide show, didn't presume to be more important or newsworthy or insightful than anybody else. He just told personal stories people could identify with.

I remembered that, and the response to my own personal comment in my last column, when I took over "For Starters" again in 1985. At first I felt a little self-conscious writing so personally. But indeed, readers seemed to like anecdotes they could identify with.

The response has overwhelmed me, and I have Eric to thank.

In considering putting several columns in one volume, I discovered that many of them constitute a memoir in snippets. I had not set out to chronicle my existence, and these are—for the most part—just slices of life. But as I arranged and rearranged them for sensible flow, I found a chronology from my own experience that transcended the dates of the columns. I have arranged them to be read in order, though that is more important in the first section than the second.

People have their favorites. The column drawing the most response was "Of Scandals and Hedges," page 133, which resulted in a book, *Hedges: Loving Your Marriage Enough to Protect It* (Wolgemuth & Hyatt).

"A Dad by Any Other Name," page 161, and "Ask No Quarter," page 125, also drew gratifying reactions, as did "A Few More Days," page 19, and "Stop on a Dime," page 145. If I had to choose a favorite, it would be "Love on a Winter's Night," page 153.

The collection begins and ends with stories of children influenced for Christ by their parents. It is dedicated to two dear compatriots, whose story is found in "Forever Friends," page 173.

I feel constrained to clarify, because some care about such things, that I will accept no income from this book. The column is a delight to write, and I have done it on Moody time as part of my work, so I take the recasting of it into book form as a compliment and the only recompense I need.

Whether you've been a *Moody Monthly* reader and have seen many of these before or you're new to me and my soapbox, I hope you will find something of value here.

A MEMOIR
IN SNIPPETS

1

'A Few
More Days'

At times I wish I looked forward to the return of Christ with as much excitement as I looked forward to a delivery when I was seven years old.

I feel the weight that we may be in the last days. The apostle Paul felt the same, nearly two thousand years ago. We could be another two thousand years from the return of Christ, yet we must spread the gospel fast, just in case.

What is it about that most wondrous of all promises that makes some hope it doesn't happen until after next week's ball game or until they are married, have children, get promoted, accomplish something?

Scripture is clear that to be with Christ "is far better," but that remains a mystery. Even with all the scholars in Christendom, we know little about heaven. We know what will be there (light and splendor) and what will not (darkness), and we know we will have glorified minds and bodies (I can get excited about that). I'm confident we won't be bored, but try explaining that to a six-year-old who doesn't want to go to heaven because "I like *my* bed."

I admire those who genuinely look forward to the return of Christ or their own home-goings because they long to be with their Savior. They look forward with eager anticipation, waiting, watching for that great day.

I have waited for good things in my life, sometimes for things that never came. Some came and didn't satisfy. But never have I waited and anticipated and hoped and prayed for anything the way I did when I was seven.

My dad was a city police officer with a wife and three boys, and although we were not poverty-stricken, we enjoyed few extras. Someday I'll have to ask Dad how he managed it. He either saved (likely), borrowed (unlikely), or got a bonus (implausible). Anyway, he piled us into the car and we went to a shop where we looked at used bicycles. We didn't hope for the gorgeous new ones; we didn't even beg. It isn't that we were that wonderful; we were simply realistic.

Somewhere in the sales pitch the bike man allowed that if Dad could see his way to purchase three brand-new Schwinns, it would cost him very little more than three good used bikes. Eyes wide, mouths agape, we heard Dad tell the man he had a deal.

Big brother Jim was fitted for a full-sized red one. Jeff got an identical one, but green. Mine was identical to Jeff's but small. Beauties, they would be sent to our home the next day.

When the eggshell blue pickup arrived, the two big bikes were delivered. It would be "a few more days" for mine. Did anyone understand what that meant to a seven-year-old?

For days I raced home after school to see if my bike had arrived. More than once I chased a blue pickup down our street, only to see it pass our house. One Saturday I sprinted till I was out of breath and saw the truck pull into our driveway and leave—with my bike aboard—because no adult was home to take the delivery.

That was the worst. I didn't know bike trucks didn't make Sunday deliveries. But when I got home from school Monday, Mom sent me to the garage. There it was, lined up with Jim's and Jeff's. But still I couldn't ride it. I had forgotten that bikes were delivered without air in the tires.

I walked the bike around, not allowed to sit on it till Dad got home and could run it up to the filling station for air. Then I rode so much during the half hour before dark that I was delightfully sore for days. All that waiting and hoping, the disappointments, and the final delay had made my treasure only more cherished.

More than thirty years later I remember the deep ache of longing for that promise and the joy of its coming. That's the way I want to feel about the coming of Christ.

2

AND TO ALL
A GOOD NIGHT

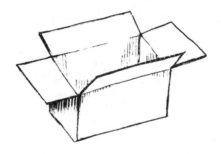

After Christmas many years ago, three elementary-school-aged boys played with their new toys until they were tired of them—three days or so.

Their mother brought an empty cardboard box into the dining room, sat the boys down, and told them of underprivileged kids at a local boys' orphanage who each got a piece of fruit, a candy bar, a comb, and a cheap toy in a standard package.

"Merry Christmas," one of the brothers said with sarcasm.

Their mother nodded, brows arched. "How about we give some of those guys a Christmas they won't forget?"

They sat silent. She continued.

"Let's fill this box with toys that will make Christmas special. We'll do what Jesus would do."

One of the brothers had an idea. "With all my new stuff, I don't need all my old stuff!"

He ran to get armloads full of dingy, dilapidated toys, but when he returned, his mother's look stopped him. "Is that what Jesus would do?"

He pursed his lips and shrugged. "You want us to give our new stuff?"

"It's just a suggestion."

"All of it?"

"I didn't have in mind all of it. Just whatever toys you think."

"I'll give this car," one said, placing it in the box.

"If *you* don't want that," another said, "*I'll* take it."

"I'm not givin' it to you; I'm givin' it to the orphans."

"I'm done with this bow and arrow set," another said.

"*I'll* take that," another chimed in.

"I'll trade you these pens for that model."

"No deal, but I'll take the pens and the cap gun."

The boys hardly noticed their mother leave the room. The box sat there, empty and glaring. The boys idly slipped away and played on the floor. But there was none of the usual laughing, arguing, roughhousing. Each played with his favorite toys with renewed vigor.

One by one the boys visited the kitchen. It was a small house and that was the only place their mother could be.

Each found her sitting at the table, her coat and hat and gloves on. Her face had that fighting tears look. No words were exchanged.

The boys got the picture. She wasn't going to browbeat her sons into filling that box. No guilt trips, no pressure. It had been just a suggestion. Each returned to play quietly, as if in farewell to certain toys. And to selfishness.

A few minutes later, their mother came for the box. The eldest had carefully and resolutely placed almost all his new toys in it. The others selected more carefully but chose the best for the box.

Their mother took the box to the car without a word, an expression, or a gesture. She never reported on the reception of the orphans, and she was never asked.

Several years of childhood remained, but childishness had been dealt a blow.

3

YOUR GOD IS A JEALOUS GOD

S ome writers call it snake oil theology, our self-
centered evangelical pop culture of self-help
books and seminars. Carole Mayhall warns that
God's definition of boasting is a universe apart from
our understanding.

All I know is, God is jealous. He hates pride. He has
a way of putting us in our places.

Sometimes He's kind enough to nudge us with something humorous. Like the time my eight-year-old was showing off my published works to the neighborhood kids and announced, "These are all the books my dad has read!"

They were impressed.

A flustered admirer, upon meeting her favorite author, gushed, "Once I put your book down, I couldn't pick it up again!"

"You write books, huh?" an unimpressed man once snickered to an author. "Must take you months. You could just buy one for about ten bucks."

A noted Christian pianist relates a true story that keeps him humble. He was practicing in an empty church sanctuary several hours before a concert when the custodian charged up the back stairway and burst through the door.

"Oh, it's you," he said. "I thought some kids were up here bangin' on the piano!"

God even allows bullies to be put in their places. When I was a kid, the bully in our neighborhood was frightening and overbearing. One day, this boy (thirteen or fourteen years old at the time) was bragging about how his father let him back the family car down the driveway and then drive it back up to the garage. He did it most of the morning, up and back, up and back. He bragged about it most of the afternoon and demonstrated his ability to anyone who cared to watch.

Then my brother Jeff showed up on his brand-new, gleaming red bicycle. Nobody wanted to watch bigmouth drive his dad's car up and down the driveway anymore. The bully stood sullenly at the edge of the crowd and pursed his lips. Finally he broke in. "Only a three-speed, huh?"

Jeff raised his eyebrows and, in his quiet way, paused for effect. "Yeah, well, at least I can take it out of my driveway."

The point is, we'll all be put in our places one day. If

not now, on the judgment day. God will not be robbed of His place, His power, His honor. The day will come when every knee shall bow and every tongue confess that Jesus Christ is Lord.

Not just Christians, not just Baptists, not just fundamentalists, not just separatists, not just evangelicals. Everybody. People who are known as good. Scholars. Intellectuals. Advantage-takers. The condescenders. The selfish.

In the words of a famous sermon, it'll be payday someday. For the just and the unjust. For those who understand and those who don't.

For those who had it all figured another way and for those who believed.

The bullies, the egotists, the self-pleasers who would have their reward now will not have it later. The glory, the dominion, the power, and the bent knees belong to the jealous, holy God.

True humility, knowing where we stand with God, is a noble pursuit and can also become a vicious cycle. When you know you have reached true humility, have you then lost it because of that knowledge?

I once heard a man pray, "Lord, thrill us with who we are in You, and remind us gently who we're not."

How long will God be patient with those of us who would rob Him of glory, who would take the spotlight, who would be proud of our humility? Will He indeed "remind us gently" until the judgment day, and, meanwhile, will our reminders come in the form of humorous jabs that help the medicine go down?

Or do we run the risk of calamity by not learning this lesson?

4

YE OLDE MODERNE TRANSLATIONETH

At the Oakwood Bible Church in Kalamazoo, Michigan, we were undenominational and independent, but I wasn't aware of that until after we'd moved away when I was a teenager.

That's the way it should be, I think. Ours was an evangelical, fundamental church, and we probably even leaned toward the blindly patriotic. But we kids weren't aware of it. Our pastor preached Christ and Him crucified, and we got the basics down cold.

In the early '60s, when Kenneth Taylor came out with the *Living Letters*—precursor to the *Living Gospels, Living New Testament*, and eventually *The Living Bible*—I recall the news hitting our church like a refreshing breath of air. There was no controversy, no hand-wringing, no thought that his helpful little tool was meant to replace the *real* Bible.

It seemed everyone had a copy or two of the green and white *Living Letters*, and though it appeared to have been written for children, I recall adults carrying them around, too, and actually reading them.

All of our memorizing had been done from the King James. And while the cadence and poetic style somehow made it easier, I confess there were many verses that were stamped on my mind but not in my heart until many years later when I learned what they meant.

I spent almost three weeks in the hospital when I was eight, and my mother took advantage of the time to help me memorize the third chapter of the gospel of John.

For the most part, I understood and enjoyed the story of the religious leader Nicodemus, visiting Jesus by night. But it didn't surprise me that Nicodemus had trouble understanding what Jesus was saying.

Nicodemus was instructed to "marvel not." Let me tell you, I marveled.

The whole chapter, of course, is filled with the mysteries of God. I was content to accept and believe that one day I would understand all the talk of being born of water and of the Spirit. That wasn't as much of a problem as simply the wording and style of verse 8:

> The wind bloweth where it listeth, and thou hearest the sound thereof, but canst not tell whence it cometh, and whither it goeth: so is every one that is born of the spirit.

Had I been asked what that meant, I would have answered the way my nine-year-old did when I asked him the same question after he recited his umpteenth AWANA memory verse:

"Don't ask me!"

The key, of course, if we are going to insist that children still memorize from centuries-old translations, is to teach them what the words mean.

My dad made John 3:8 clear to me when he said, "You can hear the wind, but you can't see it." Oh.

Some new versions are closer to being word-for-word translations (a literal word-for-word translation would not be readable in English); others are considered more thought-for-thought.

All translations have their strengths and weaknesses, and people have their favorites and their pariahs. Still, we can rejoice that God has protected His inspired Word through the generations.

As you encourage your children to memorize it and meditate on it, use the translation that will stick in their minds, and explain every word.

5

REVIVAL BEGINS
IN THE MIRROR

Acommon error is to assume revival has to do with salvation. Salvation of the lost may be a result of it, but revival in the true sense is a reviving of the believer. It is a new call, a fresh commitment, a return to our first love of Christ.

Most Christians can recall an experience sometime following their conversion where they, in a sense, come back to God after a period of spiritual dryness. Sometimes the rededication experience is so meaningful, emotional, or dramatic that it may be mistaken for salvation.

As Christians, we must be careful to not emphasize experience that is not supported by Scripture. Any experience should be scrutinized in the light of the Bible, not the reverse.

Many who have been believers since their childhoods can recall many rededicatory experiences through their teen years. But there's usually one that is valid and lasting, one that "takes." Perhaps the previous encounters were merely guilt trips or tricks of your conscience. The resulting effort to perform better as a Christian was fleshly and short-lived.

But the big one, the meaningful one, was the result of your seeking God, of sincerely desiring, with the psalmist, to "create in me a clean heart."

Maybe yours came at an evangelistic meeting, a camp meeting, or through reading a book. Maybe it came as a result of your disobedience to God or of falling into sin so alarmingly or with such dire results that you were driven back to Christ through fear or sadness or guilt.

I remember mine clearly, though it was more than twenty-five years ago. I was working at a camp where a young evangelist, John Ankerberg, was to speak. He'd been one of my spiritual models, the friend of a friend, and I was secretly proud that he would actually ask me, a fifteen-year-old, what he should speak about that night.

I told him with confidence. "Phoniness. There are a lot of phonies out here this week." I was sincere. I didn't count myself among the phonies.

John recruited me to counsel the phonies, should any of them want to repent after he spoke. I was thrilled to have even been asked.

I sat in the back, ready to counsel when the time

came. I don't know when in the message that God got through to me, but suddenly I was under conviction, good ol' fashioned heart-pounding, mind-racing, guilt-ridden conviction that I had been living in sin.

And truly, I had not intended to be a phony. No, where God reached me through John's message wasn't about overt sin, rebellion, vices, or hatred. It was over my brand of secret Christianity.

I didn't run with a bad crowd, didn't do anything wrong, didn't get into trouble. But neither did anyone outside the Christian community know I was a believer.

John challenged us to say, "I'll stand for Christ by God's grace if I have to stand alone." I had made that commitment before, only this time the key was getting out of God's way and letting Him do the work.

As soon as John invited people to stand and be counted, I leaped to my feet. He said, "Counselors are already standing, ready to pray with you," and he sent a young camper my way for counseling.

If you've never tried counseling someone about your own spiritual problem while under conviction, I don't recommend it. As soon as I finished, I ran to the privacy of a friend's car and, as we liked to say it back then, "got right with God."

What refreshment! What peace of mind! What joy! And what a corresponding sense of sadness and loss that I had not been revived earlier.

6

MOM'S OLD BIBLE

L ate one night when I was a teenager, I took a good
look at my mother's old Bible. The crumbling
cover and dog-eared pages brought back
memories of bedtime prayers. I thought of Mom when
she was Mommy.

An inscription from Dad dates the Bible from
before my birth. Mom's maiden name was barely
readable on the cover.

Two references were penned onto the dirty first page. One—John 3:5—is unmistakably written by my oldest brother, Jim. The backward scrawl reminded me of those years when the old Bible was passed around, carried to church, and claimed as "mine" by three different boys. Mom didn't often get to carry the Bible herself while we were growing up, but we frequently found her reading it at home when we came in from paper routes or baseball games.

The other reference on that first page was Psalm 37:4 in Mom's handwriting. I turned to the chapter and saw that Mom had underscored the verbs in the first five verses. They admonish:

"*Fret not* thyself because of evildoers. . . .
"*Trust* in the Lord, and do good. . . .
"*Delight* thyself also in the Lord. . . .
"*Commit* thy way unto the Lord; *trust* also in him; and he shall bring it to pass."

But apparently her favorite was "Delight thyself also in the Lord; and he shall give thee the desires of thine heart."

On the next page is the inscription from Dad. "To Bonnie, in loving remembrance of October 21, 1942—Your devoted Red. Matthew 19:6." He had been nearly nineteen, she sixteen, when they were engaged. World War II and his thirty-two months in the Pacific delayed their marriage until December 1945.

I turned the next page. "Hello everybody." Jim's writing again, probably kindling someone's indignation. But the words were never scratched out, and they remain as a child's warm welcome for anyone who cares to open Mom's old Bible.

On the next page Jim wrote "The Way of Salvation" with a verse for each of five steps. Despite the inconsistent strokes of the pre-teen writer, the guidelines are still there for men of all ages who want, as Jim pointed out in step three, a "way of escape."

Scanning the pages, I noted several of Mom's markings, countless underlinings of promises and passages that look to heaven. The penciled markings had faded and the inked jottings had bled through to other pages. But the evidence remained of well-listened-to sermons and cherished hours alone in the Word.

In the back, after the concordance, the guides, and the maps, Mom listed several references to crown of joy, righteousness, life, and glory. Looking up 1 Thessalonians 2:19 showed me again that Mom loved to rejoice in the thought of Christ's return.

On the last page of Mom's Bible, she again wrote "Psalm 37:4." That last inscription is framed by the doodling of youthful hands. One of the desires of Mom's heart was that her little boys would grow up and do something more profitable with those once-small hands.

Mom's first desire, she told us, was that her four boys would make decisions to trust Christ. We have all done that. Mom still delights herself in the Lord, which is a continual encouragement for me to do something constructive with the hands that scribbled in her Bible so many years ago.

Mom's old Bible reminds me of her hands. Hands that held, spanked, mended, and wiped tears; hands that produced a magic knot in the shoelaces on my three-year-old feet.

Mom's hands turned the pages of her old Bible for me until I learned to read it myself.

7

DON'T KEEP
THE FAITH

I n high school my brother Jeff and I had finally
broken out of the spiritual doldrums and decided
to live for Christ, by God's grace, even if it meant
we were alone in a school of 2,500. It turned out we
weren't alone, and we both enjoyed meeting new Christian friends and seeing old friends come to Christ.

But I became impressed by one older friend who

seemed to have his act together. He talked a good spiritual game, even testified in church, and led singing occasionally.

Most impressive was his tract wallet. It was a big, tri-fold vinyl holder stuffed with an all-star lineup of tracts. He even had pamphlets containing entire sermons from a famous evangelist. This was no shirt-pocket wallet. It fit only in the breast pocket of a suit coat.

Every time we got together, I asked to see his tract wallet. I read those sermons and noticed on the back that others were free for the asking. I wrote to the evangelist's headquarters and asked for every sermon available.

It was a great day when those sermons arrived in the mail. I stayed up late for two or three nights, reading hundreds of sermons. They were inspiring, and I learned a lot. Then I asked my friend where I could get a wallet like his. I had never seen one before.

"You really like it?" he asked.

I said I sure did. And now I needed a convenient place for my sermon pamphlets and my own tract stash.

"You can have it," he said.

"Really? Are you serious? What will you do with your stuff?"

"You can have that, too."

It was too good to be true. I told him several times that I didn't feel right about taking it, but he knew how intrigued I was with it. He said he could get more literature and another wallet. No problem.

I cherished that wallet. I took it with me to every meeting, and at home I organized it and reorganized it until I had tracts on every subject and sermons on various topics arranged like a mini-library.

It was a few months before I realized that I had never given away anything from that wallet. I hadn't shared my faith for weeks. I was so busy maintaining my little storehouse of spiritual goodies that I had become ineffective as a witness.

Younger Christians knew about my new tract wallet, and they were as impressed with it as I had been when my friend had it. They didn't know that I wasn't living up to its potential, just as I didn't realize—until later—that I had never seen my friend really use it either.

I added to it. By the time I was a freshman at Moody Bible Institute in the fall of 1967, I also carried a tiny three-ring notebook full of pithy statements like: "You can't know how good the good news is until you know how bad the bad news is."

I showed it to my new friends. One girl seemed particularly unimpressed and kept asking kindly what its purpose was. The tracts, the sermons, the sayings were fine, she implied, but so what?

"What do you do with them?" she wanted to know.

Soon I began leaving the bulging wallet in my room. It was noticed by a friend who was impressed with it. "Don't you use it?" he asked.

"Nah."

"Would you consider letting me have it?"

I said no to that, too. I didn't want it to do to him what it had done to me. I spent that evening reading through all the stuff again. The next afternoon I stuck it in a corner of my closet and accepted the invitation of some friends whose faith was not in a wallet, not in their pockets.

Their plan was not to keep the faith, but to give it away. We hit the streets.

8

MISTY CENTENARY MEMORIES

For some reason, the events that remain clearest in our memories are not necessarily those that occupied large slices of our lives.

For instance, a two-month period following my graduation from high school remains so vivid in my mind that I'm continually amazed at the detail I can recall at will. The strangest thing is, no one monumental thing happened that summer. It's just that those brief months were pivotal in my life.

I was the third son my parents saw graduate from high school within a four-year span, and then, as now, raising a family was expensive. There was no way they could finance our college educations. Financially, we were on our own.

The late 1960s were the days when you could still finance a whole year of college with a summer of construction work—if you were lucky enough to land a job.

Our community was in the middle of a housing boom, and I was hired as a laborer. In more than twenty years of full-time work since then, I have never enjoyed a more accurate title.

The uniform was construction boots, blue jeans, and a T-shirt. For the first two weeks, suntan lotion was a necessity. By the third week, I was brown and leathery like everyone else, brown hair bleached almost blond. I feared manual labor. Mowing the lawn or cleaning the garage were challenges. To me, work was sports writing, covering ball games, shooting pictures.

"Laborer" was a means to an end. It would pay for the year I wanted to spend studying at Moody Bible Institute.

I can remember lacing up my boots. My dad dropping me at the site on his way to the office. The coarse men. Their language. The endless hours. Carrying wood. The heavy equipment. Thirst. Hunger. Dust. Mud.

Just two months, yet enough money for a year of college and memories to last a lifetime. Maybe I knew it was my last summer at home. Maybe work that hard was so foreign to a suburban kid that I remember it as if it were a sentence.

Yet the memories aren't all bad. I remember getting used to it. Being proud of the tan so deep it told the world I worked outdoors. Even having enough energy to play ball or run with my friends after work, something I thought I'd never be able to do again.

The summer I thought would never end ended so suddenly that it seemed the experience shouldn't really be over yet. But it was time to start at Moody.

I'd been to the Institute before. We lived within easy driving distance, and friends had attended. But there was something lump-in-the-throat about my parents pulling up out in front. It's just a brief flash now, a few seconds from the billion-plus seconds I've lived, but it seems like yesterday.

I wasn't aware of the history of the place, the heritage. Not really.

I lived in one of the oldest dorms and sneaked around in the original building with my friends after dark (it was torn down later to make room for Culbertson Hall), but the legacy of Dwight Lyman Moody and the citadel of the faith he originated had to grow on me.

It never entered my head that I might be working there years later during the centenary celebration. (That possibility was likely lost on my dean as well.)

Yet the friends made, the lessons learned, the godly influences are as vivid in my memory as that first summer out of high school. I've worked at Moody more than a third of my life, yet it's that freshman year that dominates my memory.

A slice of life, a process of growing up, the impact of a place and its people on a young life can never be forgotten. Imagine the collective memories represented by those who have studied here since 1886!

To the thousands who attended MBI, or worked here, or both, the celebration of one hundred years of the blessings of God on an institution takes on a new meaning.

It does for me.

9

LOW-KEY
ANGEL

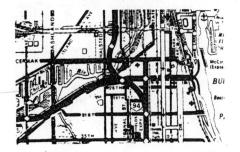

I f I hadn't bought my first house from the man, he might not remember me at all. I'll be surprised if he remembers the incident I am about to repeat. Gary Havens, a married student at Moody Bible Institute when I was a freshman during the 1967-68 school year, was editor of the student newspaper. I spent a lot of time in that quaint, cluttered office, upstairs from the

Sweet Shop and next to the barbershop in a building that no longer exists.

Gary was quietly impressive. He was always dressed up, like a real adult at work. That made the rest of us want to dress appropriately, too. Gary took his job seriously, and it rubbed off. We wrote and edited and thought and planned better when we worked at it, rather than when we played at it.

Though Gary could be blunt and wasn't afraid to forthrightly disagree, and though he didn't allow silliness to go on too long, we had fun. We were part of something. His standards were high. Nothing done halfway was acceptable. No one got away with treating the *Moody Student* like a typical college newspaper.

At the end of the year, that volume of the paper received several prestigious honors. More important, those of us who worked there took good work habits with us into careers and ministries.

Yet the incident I think of when Gary Havens comes to mind has nothing to do with journalism or professionalism. It has more to do with compassion and sensitivity.

During my first month as a student, I turned eighteen. Had that occurred while at home, my parents would have seen to it that I register for the draft. As a student, I was in little danger of being called into service, yet the law stated that I had to register in person.

A suburban kid, I was new to Chicago. Moody was a cocoon against the big city. When practical Christian work assignments took me onto the streets, buses, and subways, I was in a group, following the leader. No groups went to register for the draft. Before your birthday rolled around, your job was to get there and do your red-tape thing in the bureaucratic jungle.

I don't recall how Gary learned of my impending birthday, but one day, without making a big deal of it, he reminisced about his first confusing months in Chicago. He'd had to learn the streets, the mass transit routes, the business end of things. He must have seen a look in my eyes that betrayed the terror I would never admit.

He spoke casually. "Let me know when you have to go, and I'll run you over there."

He would run me over there? Could he have any idea how freeing those words were to my spirit? I thanked him nonchalantly, wanted to embrace him, to exult in my good fortune. The dread of this very grown-up experience was ominous enough without the trauma of simply trying to get there.

When the day came, Gary and his wife drove me to the Selective Service System office. Without condescending or belittling me, Gary walked me through the process, explaining, asking questions I would not have thought to ask, making it painless.

Before I knew it, it was over. My card—which I still have—was secured. I was legal. During the next couple of years I would still have to endure a few of the humiliating entrance examining physicals. But Gary had made the first part easy.

In the ensuing years he counseled me on when to stay or to leave an employer, sold me my first house when he and his family moved, and then lost touch. I grew up and learned the city, and now I enjoy the challenge of negotiating the maze—physical and bureaucratic.

Though it's been more than twenty years, I still remember how foreign it all was to me. And how grateful I was—and am—to Gary Havens.

10

'DON'T GO DOWN THERE'

In April of 1968 I was an eighteen-year-old college student confined to an inner-city campus because of violence in the streets.

Martin Luther King, Jr., had been assassinated, and blacks in Chicago ghettos—and all over the United States—reacted with a rage born of frustration and helplessness.

After groaning about being campused, we adolescents found ways to entertain ourselves and make life difficult for our resident advisers. We enjoyed the feeling that we were all suffering together, and we actually had fun.

We rigged up a pie tin full of flour outside the elevator so a friend of ours was whitewashed when the door opened. He played it to the hilt, acting appropriately indignant.

You see, we really had little idea what was going on outside. We had heard reports of fires and riots and looting and National Guard troops. But the sirens sounded far away. There was nothing to see on LaSalle or Wells Streets, just north of the Loop.

And so we played.

I had sentry duty on the fourth floor landing of Smith Hall as my compatriots tipped a garbage pail full of aluminum cans over the railing on the seventh floor. (I was intrigued that a couple of hundred cans fall silently, except for a slight tinkling as they brush each other in the air.) A second later they hit the basement floor like an atomic bomb.

Of course, that brought the authorities running. I hid in the prayer room. When a resident adviser burst in, I assured him, "They're not here!" He thanked me and ran off. I took the stairs to the roof.

Stepping out onto a small balcony, I could see the city from a new vantage point. Streets were closed. I was surprised to be able to hear the soft clicking of the stop lights at Chicago Avenue and LaSalle as they changed for cars that never came.

To the south and west I heard sirens and craned my neck to see the inky sky lit up with dozens of fires. From LaSalle I heard the roar of engines and spun around in time to see a parade of military vehicles charging south, their massive, ugly bodies lined up on the double yellow line.

What was inside now seemed trivial and immature.

I felt a need to be out where the real action was. This was new to everyone, and to one born after World War II, it was big stuff. I wanted to experience it, to know what it was really all about.

So I did something stupid. I took my radio press pass (I helped out in the newsroom part time) and went out. A supermarket was ablaze a few blocks away. I seemed to be the only white civilian on the streets. The looks in the eyes of the crowd running toward the fire is something I will never forget.

A blue and white squad car carrying four cops, every window duct-taped with huge Xs, slowed as it approached me. The front window came down and a pale officer spoke, "Don't go down there."

Perhaps he was cautioning me for my own safety. I waited until the squad car pulled away, then I kept walking. The cops circled the block and slid to the curb beside me. This time the officer pointed a shotgun out the window.

"Don't go down there."

That time he explained it to me better.

When I got back to the dorm, our prank had been found out and my friends lectured. I took a lot of needling for having been unaccountably absent when judgment came. Yet my own sentence had already been delivered.

By having been out where I shouldn't have been, by encountering fear and danger and grief so real I could taste it, I had been awakened to the difference between flour whitewashes, aluminum can bombs, and the real things. Maybe we could all have fun again some other night.

11

LESSONS
LEARNED EARLY

At eighteen I struck up a friendship with the assistant manager of a fast-food place. He was a bright-eyed, open sort of a guy. Spiritual things never came up, but I looked for openings.

One day his face was lit up like noon in June. "Have I got something to tell you! It's the greatest thing I've ever heard of, and I'd be no friend if I didn't share it with you. You've got to come with me to a meeting tomorrow night."

"Well, sure, but what—"

"Just say you'll come."

I was convinced he had become a Christian, and I was depressed. Not for him, of course, but for me. This guy was more excited than I had ever been.

I told my dad—a police chief—and asked if he'd go with me. "I think I'd better," he said. "It's as likely a scam as anything. This guy naive? Interested in getting rich quick?"

"Probably, but Dad, he was as excited as a new believer."

"He *is* a new believer. But in what?"

We rode with my friend. And Dad was right. It was a pyramid selling scheme. Your average Joe, with a little work, a little luck, a little investment, and enough relatives could make a shade under $105,000 a year selling gyroscopes that would keep your car from fishtailing. Honest.

It sounded so good, such a sure thing, that I didn't know how anybody could pass it up. I wondered where I would come up with the money and how many my dad would buy. I could see why my friend was so excited. These people put Christians to shame.

When the pitch was over, the sales force took over. "How many would you like, sir?"

Dad was masterful. "None for me, thanks," he said.

The young salesman thought he had been prepared for every objection. "If you have any questions about the product, I can answer them."

"No questions."

"If you need financing, we can arrange that. Let me start you with one on a no-risk, fully guaranteed, money-back basis." He slid the order form under Dad's nose.

"No, thank you."

"You don't want to make $105,000 a year?"

Dad looked him in the eye and smiled. "I'm not motivated by great amounts of money."

Now *there* was one he hadn't heard before. "You're not? How about just the one for yourself? Do your family a favor and keep yourself safe. Keep your own car from fishtailing."

"My car doesn't fishtail. I drive slowly in bad conditions."

That valuable lesson has protected me against irrepressible sales people ever since. When they learn I'm not motivated by money, they have nowhere to go, unless their product truly is more important than the money we can both make off it.

On the way home in a steady drizzle I learned another lesson. My friend's car was equipped with "the product."

"Watch this," he said, gunning the accelerator as he turned a corner. The car spun completely around in the street.

He was red-faced, and we were silent for the next several minutes until my friend spoke. "Chief Jenkins," he said, "if you're not motivated by money, what *are* you motivated by?"

What an opening.

"I consider my life worth nothing to me, if only I may finish the race and complete the task the Lord Jesus has given me—the task of testifying to the gospel of God's grace" (Acts 20:24, NIV*).

* *New International Version.*

ON THE
SOAPBOX

12

FATAL
CHOICE

Irecently read in *Time* magazine's Behavior column a piece titled "Could Suicide Be Contagious?" It told of a trio of deaths of Bryan High School students in Omaha that provoked "questions and fears."

The three students committed suicide within five days of one another. Of course, the student body was traumatized, and school counselors had full schedules.

The students had not been friends; their deaths were not the result of a suicide pact. Psychologists like to call multiple suicides "clusters" but admit they know very little about them.

While some clustered suicides may be coincidental, others, according to *Time*, "may be self-dramatizing efforts to capture the same outpouring of sympathy that surrounded an earlier death."

Regardless, *Time* says suicide is the third leading cause of death in adolescents and young adults. The rate of suicide among fifteen- to nineteen-year-olds tripled after 1958. That it has begun to level off is of little solace. Leveling off as the third leading cause of death in that age category still leaves it as the most critical concern among people who care about teenagers. Teen suicide *is* contagious, because Satan is the author of death, and his spirit pervades such scenes.

Once I stood outside a home where a mass murder had taken place. The bodies had not yet been removed, and the murders were less than twenty hours old. And yet, though I was not inside and could not see the grisly evidence, the presence of evil was so real that everyone felt it.

A few years ago, my family lived in a Chicago suburb where a neighbor fascinated my kids. When he came home from work, his children jumped and screamed and hugged him. My own son told me, "I wish I had a dad like him."

That could have wounded me, had I not long since decided to become such a fixture around my own home that my arrival would be taken in stride. I'd rather my kids remember a dad who was always there for them than one whose arrival was noteworthy.

My wife and I knew the sad truth about the neighbor. I'll call him George. His kids were so glad to see him when he showed up, because he rarely did. He had a good job, but he often went two or three nights without returning home.

When George did arrive, he had gifts for everyone to make up for having been away. And these weren't business trips. His wife didn't know where he'd been either—until she got bills from bars and massage parlors.

My wife and I discussed George until well into the night one evening. I pontificated that he needed God, needed a spiritual anchor in the universe, needed peace, joy, hope, and a reason for living.

"How do we tell him?" Dianna asked.

I outlined a long process of earning the right to be heard, meeting with George's family informally, socially, really getting to know him. It all made sense. "He needs to be desperate before he'll come to us for help or before he thinks anything we have to say is valid," I said.

We slept well, having decided to get together with George and his wife "sometime soon," just to break the ice.

The next morning I was called to the phone from a meeting. It was Dianna. "George's wife found him in the garage with the car running. He left a note on the kitchen table."

I could hardly speak. "Why do we always wait?" I managed. "Why do we *always* wait?"

It *is* contagious. It *is* epidemic. George *was* desperate. Know any Georges? Don't wait.

13

OF STICKERS, AND GATES OF SPLENDOR

They say it's a sign of age when you can think of nothing more delicious than a free half hour for a little uninterrupted reading. I must be getting old.

When only in my mid-thirties, I looked forward to a family vacation for more reasons than being able to spend whole days with my wife and boys. I'd also be able to read until the wee hours when everyone else was asleep. The next day I could sleep in or catch a nap at the beach.

See? Age.

I read anything and everything I could find that had been left in the apartment we were renting at the Maranatha Bible Conference Center in Muskegon, Michigan. Someone had left several Christian books, classics, and a few contemporary works as well. I was in heaven.

I speed read a half dozen or so—as fast as one of my vintage can speed by now—and then discovered one of those books we've all heard of and know we should have read, but I simply hadn't.

I settled in with Elisabeth Elliot's *Through Gates of Splendor* and read a few chapters a night for the next week until I was through. It's the story of her husband Jim and his four missionary colleagues, who were martyred at the hands of the Auca Indians in South America thirty years ago.

This is a book you read with a lump in your throat. You know the outcome, yet you plunge ahead, aware of the irony of men speaking and writing of potential danger and their relative readiness to sacrifice their lives, to meet God, to change residences. Not long into the reading, I recalled having heard recently that Paul Santhouse, then a colleague at Moody Press, had read an old Elisabeth Elliot book that had left him feeling "slain" for several days. I knew what he meant.

I pondered the value of the book, the value of the craft of writing, the power of the printed word. Moved by the lives of people who had unreservedly sold out to Christ, I was forced to compare current evangelicalism with the firebrand faith of the '50s. Men were men and missionaries were missionaries, and Christians were more interested in how well they knew God than in how well they were known.

Will it ever again be like it was in the late '40s and

early '50s when myriad Christian organizations sprang up to share Christ as the answer to the needs of contemporary society? Are there but a few truly devout believers left, and do we merely tolerate them and relegate them to a superspiritual minority?

Would we be comfortable today around a Jim Elliot, or would we be eager to toss in a religious platitude and move on to our next amusement?

Not long after reading *Through Gates of Splendor*, I attended the Christian Booksellers Association convention in Washington, D.C. It's a four-day affair where publishers make book dealers aware of what's new.

There is always good and bad at these events, of course, and sometimes it's difficult to avoid cynicism. Ten years ago I was introduced to Christian witnessing T-shirts (some available even for dogs!), and since then we have seen Scripture tea and even Scripture cookies.

We also saw wonderful products, books and tapes that may one day be considered classics like *Through Gates of Splendor*.

The low light of the convention for me, however, came when I passed a booth advertising Christian bumper and window stickers for your car. Some were harmless I suppose, if you see value in anonymous, shirt-sleeve witnessing.

But other selections included "God loves blondes," "God loves Amway distributors," and even "God loves bachelors and so do I."

Ah, the power of the printed word. We have taken the medium God chose to reveal His Word to the world, and in the case of Elisabeth Elliot, we have glorified Him with it.

In the case of the stickers, I fear we have shown what truly idiotic heights we can reach.

Or maybe it's just my age.

14

HERE IT IS SEPTEMBER

Three days. Inside three brief days I was brought face to face with my mortality in harmless but persistent ways.

First, I received an invitation to the twentieth reunion of my high school graduating class. *Twenty*? I've lived two years longer *since* I graduated than I had *when* I graduated. Then why do I feel less sure of myself now than then?

Will I attend? Nah. I'm not into cash bars, aging rock bands, and dancing. The one buddy I hung around with I still see occasionally at Awana functions. Funny, he looks his age. I look like his father. High school was a lot of years and too many pounds ago.

The day after receiving that encouraging piece of mail, I attended the wedding of my first niece. C'mon! I remember when this girl was born! Her father is my big brother, not that much older than I, and he's a father-in-law? I remember when he was eight!

The wedding was held at the church where I grew up. I saw friends I hadn't seen for nearly twenty-five years. I recognized them immediately. They looked like their parents. How must I have looked to them?

I came back from the wedding in time for a funeral. The man was a mentor, a model. I met him at a writers conference. He was an old pro then. Forty-five. I was twenty-two.

Somehow, I thought of him as much older then than now. He died young. He was sixty. His was a godly legacy, but such a short one when you think about it. Yet I'd have to live twice as long to accomplish so much.

What affects me so deeply about these nagging reminders of the unrelenting passing of time is the perspective it puts on history. I find it amusing when the eyes of people born in the '60s glaze over at the mention of the assassination of John Kennedy, the Beatles phenomenon, Vietnam.

Do you realize that Watergate was twice as long ago to our kids than World War II was to my generation when we were in grade school in the '50s? Think of that! When my father, at roughly my current age, spoke of Pearl Harbor, of Iwo Jima, of Hiroshima, of the end of the war, he was speaking of something twice as recent to him than my high school graduation is to me now. World War II was less than ten years old.

74

Twenty years ago, I graduated from high school. Twenty years before then, the war had just ended. Skeletal survivors of the Nazi death camps had just been freed. Twenty years before that, Babe Ruth hit sixty home runs, and the stock market hadn't even crashed.

It was so recent. So recent. And it's worse heading the other way, isn't it? High school graduation seems like yesterday, and twenty years from now I'll be pushing sixty. I hope. My three little boys will be grown, likely married, fathers. I'll be married to a grandmother.

Someone explained to me once that time accelerates as you get older because each succeeding year is a smaller fraction of your total. Makes sense. Remember how a school day seemed like years and a school year seemed like forever? Such nine-month segments now simply cause people to say, "Seems like yesterday was New Year's. Here it is September."

Here it is September (1987). I'll be thirty-eight when it's over. People older than that think I'm silly for feeling old, when they'd just as soon trade places. In many ways, I still feel like a kid, still getting to know my wife after nearly seventeen years of marriage. But I'm no kid anymore. The mirror doesn't lie.

Life is fun and funny, but melancholy when it breezes by. When I shake my head at the vapor that has already appeared for half an instant and is beginning to fade away, all I want to do is to remind myself that I could very well live again as long as I've already lived.

And I want above all else to redeem the time.

15

ON THE
FRONT LINES

Think about people who are on the front lines, in the trenches. I'm not talking about Nicaragua or Lebanon; I'm talking about the battle with principalities and powers.

The shepherds and the wise men were on the front lines. Their experience was firsthand. No one had to convince them of anything or persuade them to do anything. When God tells you to follow a star, you follow the star. When an angel tells you what you'll find in Bethlehem, you go to Bethlehem.

Today, we can still look to a few who are sold out to Christ, who live on the ragged edge of faith, who look to God for sustenance, for leading, for support, for survival.

I can't say I've been much of a front-liner over the years, though the experience is available to me and to any Christian who is willing to make himself available to God. It has, however, been my privilege to write about front-liners.

Probably the most dynamic, most inspiring, and most faithful servant I have had the opportunity to write about is Sammy Tippit. When I met him, he was just twenty-five.

At that time, Sammy was a Southern boy with a thick accent that was never so pronounced as when he lovingly talked about "Jayzus Chroist."

He had dropped out of his senior year of college because of a burden for lost souls. He had to preach, to witness, to hit the streets, to live on faith. God had called him, and he couldn't sit another minute in the classroom, though he had been a brilliant student.

He and his wife, Tex, carried a cross to Washington, D.C., during the height of the Jesus Movement, drawing interest and taking advantage of the curiosity of young people to preach Christ everywhere they went. Scores came to God.

Sammy felt led to Chicago, where he lived in a big house with several other couples. God's Love in Action, Inc., ministered to street people there, witnessing, singing, and preaching.

Once he was arrested for disturbing the peace because he was passing out tracts in front of a nightclub. Waiting for the trial, he fasted and prayed at the civic center, winning more and more people to Christ.

The Moody Bible Institute lawyer procured another Christian lawyer for him, and he was acquitted of the charge. The ministry continued, the couple subsisting on money from Sammy's many speaking engagements and donations.

Sammy was challenged by the stories of pioneers of the faith who depended upon the Lord and never asked anyone for money, and he patterned his ministry that way. He's almost embarrassed to tell of the countless times God provided just the right amount at the perfect moment, because he would rather Christians live their lives by the Word of God than by someone else's experience.

He's been ministering behind the Iron Curtain for years, with just a few breaks of a year or two each when he served pastorates in the States. A church he pastored in Germany exploded with growth during his brief time there.

A few years ago he felt led to leave a comfortable Texas pastorate to return to the front lines of living by faith. Once again he's on the streets, in the churches behind the Iron Curtain and on several continents, living hand to mouth, counting on the Lord for everything. He and his wife have two children, and life is tougher as a family called to a faith ministry. But Sammy has never been more motivated, more excited.

16

PEACE
AT THE BORDER

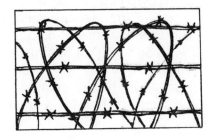

I t happened in 1986, yet I remember the fear as if
it were yesterday.

Sammy Tippit and I had alternated driving
a rented Volkswagen all day through Hungary from
Austria. Our plan was to cross the border into Romania
sometime before midnight.

My then eleven-year-old son, Dallas, was asleep in the back, his mind and body ravaged by industrial strength jet lag. To him, the danger of being interrogated, detained, maybe arrested and deported to Siberia was exciting. After having slept all day, Dallas would be up all night, alert and wired for the border crossing. Having *not* slept all day, my nervousness—no, fear—would trick me into alertness long past my fatigue threshold. I would pay for this.

To Sammy Tippit, this was old hat. It would be his tenth border crossing into Romania. He had preached there many times. The idea of going with my old friend and taking my son had seemed dramatic, daring. Until now. The sky grew dark, then darker, then black. Dallas was up and full of questions. I didn't like Sammy's answers.

How long might we be detained? The shortest previous border crossing had been eight hours. Had anyone ever been refused entry? Yes, two laymen who tried to get in a second time were turned away; they were told they had been blacklisted because of the activities last time with Sammy. Yet Sammy was allowed through.

As we left Hungary, a border guard searched our car while we stood stamping and steam-breathing in the night air. In a friendly tone, but in a language I didn't understand, the Hungarian guard nodded to Dallas and said to Sammy, "Ah, a child."

Sammy responded in the same language, "Yes, a child."

"Oh, you speak Romanian?"

"Very little," Sammy said. It had been a *faux pas*. An American in a car rented in the West, speaking Romanian. When the guard left, Sammy predicted he would warn the Romanian border guards a hundred yards away. My fear mounted.

The guards at the Romanian border were stereotypes. Blocky, stern, flat-faced men in uniforms, sarcastic, slow-moving, condescending, and heavily armed. One came straight to the driver's side and greeted Sammy in Romanian. It was then that Sammy knew why God had allowed a small error at the crossing out of Hungary. He was on alert. Though he knew enough Romanian to return the greeting, he looked blankly at the guard.

My stomach knotted as the man glared at Sammy, then slowly turned and walked away. We waited in the car for two more hours. Car after car ahead of us was turned away, only one of thirteen allowed to proceed. Soon it would be our turn to be searched, questioned, papers and periodicals examined, every inch of the car and our luggage combed.

I promised Dallas that I would not allow us to be separated. No separate searches, no separate interrogations, no taking my eyes off him. Excitement danced on his face; the precautions were for me, not for him.

"You're not nervous at all, are you?" I asked Sammy.

"I was earlier," he admitted. "The drive across Hungary, the closer we got, the more I was concerned."

"We can't get closer than this," I said, "But you're at peace. I can tell."

The windows were up against the cold. We were fogged into our own world, speaking softly. "If God wants us in Romania," Sammy whispered, "no one will be able to keep us out. If He wants us there, we'll get there. If He doesn't, we won't."

We spent ten good days there.

17

FUN JUNKIES, BEWARE

We evangelicals have become a nation of fun junkies, always looking to add creature comforts to our environments. If there's anything that will cure us, it's a trip behind the Iron Curtain.

When my eldest son, Dallas, was eleven, he and I went to Romania. The trip, with evangelist Sammy Tippit of San Antonio, Texas, pastor Gary Maroney of

Portland, Oregon, and layman Joe Davis of Graham, Texas, was to be for me a fact-finder, an eye-opener.

It sure was.

Sammy, Gary, and Joe were there to preach in churches. I would share briefly, but chiefly observe. My hope for Dallas was that he would get a view of real life, life behind the Iron Curtain.

Still suffering from jet lag and fatigue, we're both still trying to get a handle on our emotions, our thoughts, our impressions. Our brief stay in Eastern Europe saw us afflicted by sensory overload that may take years to sort out.

The first church Sammy preached to was in a small town where the people seemed to have a deep joy but also a deep sense of sadness and frustration with daily life. Neither Dallas nor I had ever spoken through an interpreter before, and it was fun to communicate with brothers and sisters in Christ with whom we shared only that bond.

Gary's and Joe's brief messages were effective and meaningful, and the Lord used Sammy's powerful preaching to bring several to Christ. The local pastor was a weary laborer known for defending the rights of the citizens against the senselessness of the secret police.

I asked him if anyone but Christians were happy in this town. He struggled with the concept of happiness.

"It is not an issue here," he concluded. Happiness was not a goal, and not obtainable anyway. Joy was expressed in a smile and a greeting of "peace" (pronounced pah-chey) between believers. Poignant truth from the pulpit elicited weeping. Happiness was not an issue.

This is a land where people stand in line for a kilo of beef per month. That's 2.2 pounds. Think of it. How long would you last on the equivalent of a half pound of butter a month? A decent salary approximates $250 a month. One in ten wage earners owns a car, and all the cars are identical except for color.

Virtually everyone lives in cramped apartments, short of money, short of food, bereft of mobility (should you be fortunate enough to own a car, you can go as far as ten liters of fuel will take you each month). Power is conserved. Streets are dark. Buildings are colorless. If there is an equivalent to our Environmental Protection Agency, it is not working. Pollution blinds and suffocates.

It's dark inside and outside. Public buildings are not heated. Any Romanian who speaks with a foreigner must report it to the secret police: names, dates, subject matter. Outsiders are followed, their inside contacts harassed. Our brief meeting with one pastor in his home was interrupted by a phone call from the secret police. He was required to come in immediately and report on his visitors.

Depressing. Oppressive. All my life I have heard and repeated cliches about how easily we take our freedoms for granted. Being there overwhelmed me. I never felt so rich, so free, so wasteful, so extravagant.

Where revival has touched cities in Romania, the picture is different. Christians are bolder, churches are packed fuller. The Second Baptist Church of Oradea began a Sunday evening service by kerosene lamp and an independent generator for microphones and platform lights.

More than three thousand packed the sanctuary, jamming every pew, every aisle, every corridor, every room in the darkness. They stood for two hours, eyes shining, faces expectant. Fire marshals in the United States never would have allowed it.

The secret police in Romania couldn't stop it.

18

TV: An Epitaph
for Values

I am not much of a television watcher anymore. A
few years ago, when our boys were very small,
my wife, Dianna, and I decided to neither fix nor
replace our wounded television. For a couple of years
we went without.

I could recite the typical litany of improved family
communications, more reading, more table games, less

hassle. All true. I'm not a militant who encourages every family to withdraw cold turkey from TV forever, but two couples I know well have been without it for years, and they have bright, productive, happy children.

We came back to television slowly. A friend gave me one of those tiny, hand-held jobs with a screen about an inch square. My wife still laughs at the memory of my brother, my dad, and me cheek-to-cheek trying to watch a heavyweight title fight. When my son tried to watch twenty-two football players and a half dozen referees on that tiny field of vision, we knew it was time to rethink our position.

We decided that our hiatus from television had been a good thing and that it had broken an addiction. Now we could own a TV and enjoy it sensibly. Our plan was to buy a nice television set, then resolve to be *very* selective about what we watched. I know what you're thinking, and I probably couldn't have kept that resolution either, had it not been for my wife.

It amuses her to hear people say they can't control the television or what the kids watch. Woe to a child with my surname who does not secure permission before engaging the cathode ray tube. They watch only what and when we say.

We put our new television in the basement, where it had to thaw before it could even think of warming up. Want to watch the Winter Olympics? Dress for them, then head downstairs. Even in our new house, where it's cold downstairs only because we want it that way, we choose far in advance what we want to watch. None of this let's-see-what's-on business.

So, what do we watch? Specials, sports, news, educational programs, the occasional game show (the ones based on intelligence, not luck), and the *very* occasional family-oriented sitcom (you know how rare those are).

Our TV is off more than it's on. Watching is a privilege earned by having homework, piano lessons, and chores done. The kids watch alone only if we are dead sure of program content. It's amazing how much discussion is necessary even after educational shows, which generally ignore the Creator and espouse evolution.

TV is worse than ever. It's difficult to brag about watching hardly anything but sports with your kids when, in so doing, you are exposing them every few minutes to sexy advertisements extolling the virtues of alcohol.

Our favorite beer commercial to hate is the one where a hunk who looks like he came off the cover of *Gentleman's Quarterly* looks us in the eye and tells us what he believes in. Playin' hard, workin' hard, rock 'n' roll, his friends, his car, his girl, and beer. Great beer. The jingle calls it "a beer you can believe in."

There's also a car you can believe in, and a shampoo that tells you to believe in your hair.

The only way I know to fight the bad influence of TV commercials is to help the kids change the lyrics to the songs. Instead of "a beer you can believe in," they sing, "A beer you can go blind with."

Dianna has a better idea how to fight them. She knows you can't raise your kids in a vacuum, but there are days when she believes we'd all be truly better off without television. And despite the occasional great ball game or inspiring special we would miss, I fear she may be right.

19

From the Mouths of Babes

Sometimes children can be too good to be true. I know the reverse can also be the case, but let me stay on the positive side. One of my three sons once told me that the wise men brought Jesus gifts of gold, frankincense, and fur.

That was when I first became aware of how priceless are some of the treasures that come from the little ones. If you are raising or have raised children, you will identify with some of the following.

When my eldest, Dallas, was six, my wife and I overheard him giving instructions to one of his tiny soldiers. "You may die in this mission," he said, "but if you're a Christian, you'll go to heaven. In heaven you can ask Jesus for anything you want, and if it's all right with your mom, He'll give it to you."

Chad, when eight, informed me he was going to read the Bible "all the way through."

I noticed a tiny-print King James Version in his hand. "That's great, Chad," I said. "How far have you gotten already?"

"Genesis 2:9."

"Wouldn't you rather have a children's Bible, something easier to understand?"

"No," he said. "You use King James, and I memorize out of it for Awana. I'll read this."

"It's going to take you a long time."

"Oh, yeah. I'll probably be nine by the time I finish."

A few weeks later he asked me how old Abel was when he died. "I don't think the Bible tells us that, Chad. Some people think he was a young person, maybe even a teenager."

"Hm," he said. "In my Bible, he lived only about eight verses!"

Just the other day I heard him telling his little brother, "Mike, plug in the tape recorder."

"I can't, Chaddy, I can't!"

"Mike, don't you know what it says in the Bible? 'I can do all things through Christ who strengthens me.' You can do *anything*!"

That convinced Mike. He plugged in the tape recorder.

Not long ago, Chad told me the story of Solomon's life, which his Sunday school class had been studying. "He could have asked God for anything, but he asked for wisdom. Then he got everything else anyway, riches and all that."

I nodded.

"But then, Dad, you know what happened at the end of his life? He blew it. He lost everything."

"It's a sad story really, isn't it, Chad?"

He looked thoughtful.

"Yeah. You'd think out of all those wives, one of 'em would've been a Christian."

20

ANGELA UNAWARE

You can sometimes learn as much about love outside the church as in. Several years ago I served
on the faculty of a writers conference noted not
only for its training but also for its emphasis on frater-
nity. Writers got to know and enjoy and love one
another during the week, and lifetime friendships were
born or cultivated.

Angela was an outsider, a newcomer drawn by the brochure's promise of a talent night. Attendees were encouraged to bring musical instruments, puppets, object lessons, a speech, a poem, whatever they wanted.

Angela arrived plain, plump, and freshly divorced. Along with her bags was a black guitar case she insisted on carrying herself. She seemed alarmed when Talent Night did not appear in the program.

"We're flexible here," she was told. "We see how the week is going, try to determine how many are interested, and then we assign a coordinator. Are you volunteering?"

"Sure!"

Angela took her job seriously. Between workshops and major sessions, she ferreted out every actor, actress, comedian, poet, orator, singer, and ventriloquist. She drew up the program, put up posters, and made announcements at every meal.

Nearly half the conferees would perform, and I knew of no one who would have missed it. Talent Night was always a hilarious highlight.

When the big night came, Angela distributed a typed program. She had organized not only the talent but also the sound and the lighting. Those who had little talent were big on chutzpah and made us laugh till we cried. Others, accomplished at tugging at heartstrings, kept us emotional.

The program went from funny to slapstick to serious, and it all led to the finale: a solo by Angela, who would accompany herself on the guitar. That black case had made us curious, and her interest in the show made us expectant.

Angela had carefully orchestrated the show by turning it gradually more serious until the end, when a woman did a monologue on motherhood and a man read a poem about the loss of a child. Then the lights dimmed, and Angela strode to a stool at stage center.

She knelt and removed her gleaming guitar, slipped

the strap over her head, and sat on the stool, crossing her legs. She rested the instrument on her knee and tuned it. I nearly laughed when her first chord was off key. Clearly the guitar was in tune. Her fingering was wrong. Her strum was not authoritative.

She winced and tried again, surrounding her notes. Her fingers trembled, her lips quivered. The introduction to her chorus was long but contained only three simple chords. It became evident that she knew only those three and had mastered none.

The more she tried, the more panic-stricken she appeared, and when she opened her mouth to sing, we could hardly hear. She was short of breath, off key, and her strumming was worse for the attention given to singing.

We agonized with her when she gave up on the guitar and tried to finish a cappella. She forgot a word and skipped it, then forgot the tune and started over.

It was then that we rallied round this sweet, tortured soul, this woman in pain who had given so much and hoped for so much. First one, then another joined her in the familiar chorus, until we were all singing, not loud but full and deep and warm.

During a pause between phrases, a man called out, "Thank you for this evening, Angela! We love you!" Three hundred stood and applauded.

Angela stood awkwardly, her hands at her sides, the guitar hanging from her neck. She tried to smile through her tears.

We had been to church.

21

THE MAGIC THAT DOESN'T DELIVER

I love Christmas. Always have. In fact, it wasn't until I had been an adult several years that I learned that loving Christmas was not universal, even among Christians.

I was shocked to learn that many people find the Christmas and New Year season the most depressing days of their lives. My source was a Christian psychologist who had studied the problem and confirmed it in many counseling sessions.

At first I doubted him. How could this be? Even enemies seem to soften at Christmastime. Belligerent clerks and delivery people seem to mean it when they wish you good cheer; people do things for each other, give things to each other, seem to love each other.

But, my friend pointed out, I grew up in a close-knit family where Christmas was a time to remember, to reflect on the birth of Christ, and to epitomize the love and servant attitudes my parents and brothers and I knew we were supposed to evidence all through the year.

Think, he said, of the person who might have grown up in a tough, demanding, unloving home. Christmas, to that person, was once idealized. In spite of all his or her troubles and feelings of insecurity, Christmas carried hope.

As a little one, that person dreamed Santa would come and make everything better. Even when the disappointing truth about Santa was revealed, there was the Christ child, and in Him was magic of some sort that makes sorrow and sadness disappear for a week or two.

Yet somehow it never lasted. No Santa, no parent, no magic could ever accomplish the permanent trick of making a person feel better about himself.

The biggest single factor, my friend the psychologist said, wasn't the pressure, though these were contributors. It wasn't even the tension of family get-togethers.

Rather, the most important contributing factor to Christmas-related depression remains disappointment. Too many expectations. Too much hope for magic that doesn't deliver.

As children we hope Santa or our parents will somehow know what we long for most. We shouldn't even have to tell them. We'll be good, we'll wish, we'll hope, we'll pray, and—just like in the classic Christmas movies—something miraculous will happen.

The problem, of course, is that as children, there are disappointments when the gifts don't match the Christmas dreams.

As adolescents, the Christmas solutions to personal crises fade or never happen at all.

And as adults, the hope for injured relationships to be healed, for prodigals to return, for broken hearts to be mended is dashed by the first week of January.

The one in pain may not even be conscious that he or she is really suffering a delayed disappointment from childhood of a doll that never appeared under the tree or a wind-up train that didn't compare with the electric model in the catalog.

The fact is, while God is in the business of healing such hurts, He doesn't act because of the date. He doesn't try to match the sappy coincidences the movie fantasies promise. He works in hearts, in minds, in souls in response to faith.

Do you suffer post-Christmas disappointment each year because of some unarticulated, maybe even subconscious dream that something will somehow be divinely fixed December 25?

Think about it, talk about it, dredge it up, pray about it, work toward it. The only magic in the Christmas season is in the turning of our thoughts to the greatest gift ever given or received: Jesus.

Concentrate on what He can do for others through you, and may this Christmas be your best ever.

22

NEVER TOO OLD TO BE SHOCKED

You think you've heard it all. Then you get your socks knocked off. Is there one tenet of evangelical Christianity you would assume is clear to any lifetime member of a Bible-believing church?

Wouldn't you assume, as I did, that if there was one thing he would have down cold, it would be the doctrine of salvation? I'm not saying he has to know any theological terms. He doesn't have to know the difference between substantiation and substitutionary atonement. Just how to get to heaven.

A few weeks ago, I wouldn't have posed the following question. But now I'm wondering just how many people in our pews have actually missed the point. It's the type of question we evangelicals use when we're clucking about what's wrong with the mainline denominations or the Catholics.

"They believe the basics," we say, "but do they really understand how to be saved?"

Now I'm wondering the same thing about people in "our kinds" of churches. Am I overreacting? I hope so, but if you want to make sure in your own church, ask people to write on a sheet of paper why they believe they are going to heaven.

The answers will astound you.

Less than a year ago, I was helping a friend counsel someone on the brink of divorce. My friend noticed a hearse go by and asked the counselee an adapted version of the "Kennedy Question" (developed by Pastor James Kennedy for his Evangelism Explosion program):

"If that were your body in that hearse, do you know you would be in heaven?"

I thought he was wasting time. I mean, the man with the bad marriage was raised in a Christian home, attended a fundamental church, had spent a couple of years in Bible college. Why not save evangelism for someone who needed it?

The answer was sure and immediate, just as I knew it would be. "Yes, I know I would be in heaven."

Good, I thought. *Let's get on with the marriage counseling.* But my friend wasn't through.

"Oh what basis?"

Again the answer was quick and sure.

"On the basis of my works."

I laughed. It was a joke, right? The classic answer

so opposite of the truth that it had to be a put-on. My laughter died when I could see in his eyes that he was serious.

Over the next several minutes we asked and probed, finally establishing that what he had understood from all those years of preaching of the gospel was that he had to earn his way into heaven.

We had the joy of showing him how that was impossible, but that Jesus had aready provided a way. He received Christ and told us recently that this past Christmas was the most exciting of this life.

I assumed he was an exception, that he had somehow slipped through the cracks. Then *USA Weekend*, a newspaper supplement, printed the results of a poll. People were asked if they thought they were going to heaven and why, and were their friends going to heaven or not.

Not suprisingly, more people thought they were going to heaven than thought their friends were. It was sad to discover that no one interviewed based his hope of heaven on the finished work of Christ.

Sadder yet was to read the comments of several who called themselves Baptists who gave the same limp reasons as their unchurched counterparts for their hope. "I try to be nice. I hope I've done more good than bad. I think God will forgive me."

We've preached it, taught it, talked about it, shared it, sung it, testified to it, and thanked God for it in prayer. But we'd better start asking around. People who shouldn't have been able to escape the truth have memorized Ephesians 2:8-9 without ever learning its message.

Ask the question. Risk offending. Don't let lifetime church people go to hell just because they were never confronted.

23

SHINE ON

Item: A young man employed by a service company decided he'd rather watch the Chicago White Sox play than spend the rest of the day working.

He drove the company truck to the ballpark, then called his office and told his supervisor that his early afternoon service call would take the rest of the day.

Fact: The young man told me that story.

Item: A young reporter interviewed a famous personality at a downtown hotel. As the reporter was preparing to leave, the celebrity noticed his parking stub.

"Let me have that stamped for you," he said.

Not understanding what he meant, the reporter followed him to the front desk, where the celebrity told the clerk, "I'm parked in the hotel lot. Can you validate this for free parking?"

"You're a guest here?" the clerk asked.

The man nodded and showed his room key to prove it. The ticket was stamped. The reporter could have parked free. But he chose to pay instead.

Fact: The reporter told me that story.

Item: A woman enjoyed lunch with an older lady and split the bill.

"Here," the older one said, "you can have the receipt for your income taxes."

"What do you mean?"

"List this as a business lunch that you paid for. You've got the receipt."

Fact: The young woman told me that story.

Item: A middle-aged man had recently moved to a big city. He parked at an expired meter, reasoning, "Even if I get a ticket, I'm changing my license plates soon. They'll never track me down."

Fact: The man told me that story.

Item: A businessman was upset that his competition was underselling him by mail. When he received the competition's catalog, he mailed in every prepaid business reply card and envelope they provided, but he ordered nothing. "They had to pay all that postage," he says with a smile.

Fact: The businessman himself told me that story.

Item: A couple celebrated their twenty-fifth wedding anniversary. Their son, a salesman, called in sick so that he could attend the party.

Fact: The couple told me that story, clearly amused at their son's resourcefulness.

Item: A young woman working as a telephone installer frequently absconded with phones left by customers who had moved.

She reported to her employer that the customers had taken the phones with them. She kept some of the phones, gave others to friends, and sold the rest.

Fact: She herself told me that story.

The saddest fact of all:

The White Sox fan is—and was at the time of his lie—an active, churchgoing Christian involved in training youth.

The famous personality is—and was at the time of her recommended deception of the IRS—on the full-time staff of an evangelical church.

The middle-aged man is—and was at the time he parked illegally—a pastor.

The anniversary couple is—and was at the time that they took delight in their son's lie—active in Christian work.

The telephone installer is—and was at the time of her theft—a professing Christian, active in her church.

"Therefore, my dear friends . . . become blameless and pure, children of God without fault in a crooked and depraved generation, in which you shine like stars in the universe" (Philippians 2:12, 15, NIV).

24

MARCH OR
QUIT SINGING

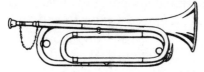

At Moody Bible Institute's Founder's Week in February of 1987, an Illinois pastor spoke on being a soldier of the cross. Bill Hybels of Willow Creek Community Church closed his quietly dramatic challenge with what I'm sure he intended as a rhetorical question:

"Who is willing to be a soldier of the cross?"

Before Pastor Hybels could bow for prayer, a young man called out. "I am!" Then another. "Me too!"

"Amen!"

"I am too!"

The atmosphere was electric, dead silent save for those men and women who had been challenged to the point where they had to express themselves. It was an emotional highlight of the week, moving even to the speaker.

It reminded me of an incident in the life of Latin American evangelist Luis Palau. As a young banking management trainee committed to Christ and eagerly studying the Word every day in Buenos Aires, Argentina, he was forced by the words in a song to evaluate himself.

From his autobiography, *Luis Palau: Calling the Nations to Christ* (Moody Press, 1983):

"My insatiable hunger for the Word of God was increasing, and I enjoyed trying to satisfy it. Then came the day we sang the hymn 'Am I a Soldier of the Cross?'

"I sang with the enthusiasm the tempo demands, but hardly thought about the words. The Lord must have used all the Bible knowledge that was being poured into me to make me sensitive to Him, because suddenly I was overcome with the meaning of the song.

Am I a soldier of the cross,
A foll'wer of the Lamb,
And shall I fear to own His cause,
Or blush to speak His name?

"The lyrics burst into my mind as if God Himself was expressing an exhortation on my heart. 'You sing of being a soldier of the cross, and yet you do nothing.' He seemed to say, 'You have never suffered for the Lord; no one has ever said a thing to you against God. Think of Mildred Cable and Francesca French—those two missionary ladies from Asia, whom your mother read to you about and whom you met several years ago.'

"My thoughts turned to those cowardly years and how little I was now doing, compared to those inspiring women. I could hardly continue singing. *What kind of coward are you?* I asked myself. *When were you ever dragged by the hair or stoned or spat upon for the gospel? You stand here and sing about being a soldier of the cross, but you are no soldier.*

"That rebuke did something for me. I began to take seriously the idea that all this Bible study and training under the elders was a call from the Lord to serve Him and even to suffer for Him, if necessary.

"It was then that I knew that I probably wouldn't be a banker all my life. And I wouldn't be a lawyer or a judge, either. I couldn't change my nation or the world through finances or law or politics or sociology. I was going to have to be a soldier of the cross or quit singing about it."

For Palau, that has meant serving on the front lines as an evangelist. The fighting is tough at times, but he says that's when he remembers the One who commissioned him:

"Sometimes you're so tired, especially if you've had a bunch of criticism, and you think, *What in the world am I doing?* You say to yourself, *You know, I really ought to go home.* But that's not a crisis, it's just being tired.

"My commitment came young. I'm always conscious of the judgment seat of Christ. And I always think, *I must respond to Jesus Christ personally, face to face at the judgment seat—that's what I'm headed for.*

"Therefore, against all criticism and other things, I must continue to do what I feel the Lord's given me to do. And I must try to persuade others around me. I must carry on."

25

KEEP
SHORT ACCOUNTS

The above was what Dr. Joseph Stowell said in January [1989] when he heard of the sudden death of former college and professional basketball superstar Pete Maravich.

In a 1974 interview with sportswriter Andy Nuzzo of the *Beaver County* (Pa.) *Times*, Maravich, then with the Atlanta Hawks, said, "I don't want to play 10 years in the [National Basketball Association] and die of a heart attack at age 40."

I saw Pete Maravich play in 1974. I was in Atlanta interviewing Pat Williams, who was the Hawks' general manager that season. Pat got me a seat at the scorer's table at courtside. I couldn't believe my luck.

I had read a story about Pistol Pete Maravich in *Sports Illustrated* when I was in college and Maravich was playing under his father, Press Maravich, at Louisana State University. After that captivating article, I followed every step of his career.

It told of a slight young man who had been committed, dedicated, and addicted to basketball his whole life. *Addicted* is not too strong a word. He literally had a basketball in his hands every moment he wasn't in class, eating, or in church. Yes, he took a basketball to bed. He lay on his back, tossing it in the air in the dark until he fell asleep with it at his side.

As his father drove down the road, Pete often leaned out the car window and dribbled. He dribbled, passed, spun, and shot the ball every possible waking moment. He grew so tired of making hundreds of shots from all over the court that he made up trick shots just for diversion. Shots that weren't even legal in a game. Like bouncing the ball off the wall and into the basket.

By giving himself to basketball, he became one of the most amazing scoring machines in the history of the game. He started on his high school basketball team when he was in eighth grade. At LSU he averaged 44 points a game for three years, a record that still stands.

He dribbled and passed behind his back, passed the ball through his legs, and sometimes even passed it between an opponent's legs. The first time up the court at the game I saw in Atlanta, he coolly dribbled across the mid-court line within feet of where I sat. In mid-dribble, without looking, he fired a bullet of a forty-foot pass behind his back into the corner where a teammate was wide open for an easy shot. More than one of the opposing Houston Rockets never saw the pass or the shot and wondered why everyone was heading back down the court.

After a ten-year pro career, Pete became an NBA Hall of Famer, but his personal life had been in shambles. A few years ago, after terrible alcohol problems and a roller-coaster existence, Pete Maravich came to Christ.

God made a jewel of his life, and he became a vibrant, dynamic witness. He and his wife and two young sons were finally at peace. Pete spoke for his Lord all over the United States. Legend has it that he once asked a group of street basketball players if he could tell them about Christ. They refused. He said, "What if I beat you, one against five?"

Had they recognized Pete, they wouldn't have agreed. During the next several minutes, he easily won the right to be heard.

Late last year his new book was released (*Heir to a Dream*, Thomas Nelson Publishers), and in January he went to California to be featured on the "Focus on the Family" radio program. Before taping, Pete played in an eight-man scrimmage with James Dobson and the others. It was the first Pete had played for almost a year due to a shoulder injury.

During a break, Dr. Dobson asked him how he felt. "I feel great," he said. Then he turned and collapsed, dead of a heart attack at age forty.

Keep short accounts.

26

SOMETHING'S WRONG SOMEWHERE

W hen Cal Thomas's *Book Burning* was released two years ago, the uninitiated may have assumed he was writing about crazies within the religious right who burned any title they found offensive.

People who knew better, those who knew of Thomas's position as a conservative and even—at that time—

an employee of Jerry Falwell, weren't surprised to find the opposite.

Secular reviewers, however, were in for a shock when they discovered that, in Thomas's view, the pseudo-liberal, secular camp was guilty of censorship.

Frankly, I didn't know what I thought of this at first. Could Thomas have been overreacting? Was he overstating the case for the sake of making his point?

As an evangelical publisher as well as an author, I knew that such tactics as overstatement have been employed by those whose views—but not methods—most of us agree with.

Now suddenly, because the issue has struck close to home, I find myself in total agreement with Cal Thomas.

In a nutshell, Thomas thinks that the real censors of our day, the ones who are truly afraid of a point of view, are those who ban evangelical books from the secular marketplace.

He cited schools, libraries, and bookstores as places where you can find anything you want on a subject—explicit sex without moral underpinnings, aberrant religions, cults, and the occult—but no evangelical Christian material.

The reasons parroted by the guardians of the public's reading habits ranged from the laughable "separation of church and state" to "we don't accept propaganda."

Look for the writings of Marx and Lenin and Trotsky and Hitler and Mao in your public library and tell me whether your librarian accepts propaganda.

The fact is, much of the secular world is afraid of the truth and its impact on young minds. And the excuses for banning such material don't stand up to the other offerings available anywhere.

If there were a shred of consistency in such decisions, it wouldn't be so troubling. But when religious writing from every corner except evangelicalism is acceptable and when mind-influencing material from every philosophical viewpoint except Christianity is disseminated, something's very wrong somewhere.

So how did I come to see that Cal Thomas was right, that he wasn't overreacting or engaging in New Right role-playing? Censorship happened to me. Twice.

I confess I'm chagrined that it had to hit me where I live before I got excited about it, but too often that's what it takes.

A portion of what I write consists of a series of fictional adventure books about a modern-day family with an overt faith in Christ. When I was asked to speak about book writing to the elementary students in a public school, the publisher of my children's series generously sent a hundred copies of the books in advance.

That gave the school librarian time to discover how harmful they would be to young minds. I was still welcome to come, as long as my talk was about writing in general. The books would not be made available to students.

I informed the school that I was unable to separate my faith from my vocation and thus had to decline the invitation. I also asked what they carried in their library that might offend me, but my question was ignored.

Recently a friend whose family has enjoyed these same books tried to donate them to her public library. They were graciously declined, she told me, because they emphasize that God is personally involved in the lives of children and that He will answer their prayers.

27

ASK NO
QUARTER

I t wasn't unusual for Mildred (not her real name)
to carry a couple of rolls of quarters in her purse;
she was assistant treasurer at her church.

Mildred was in her early sixties, devout, sweet, and
still in pain over the death of her husband six months
before. Her divorced twenty-five-year-old son of indeter-
minate sexual and pharmaceutical preference had

recently moved back home. That added stress was not good for Mildred's bad back, arthritis, and allergies.

She had long since given up trying to talk to her friends or her pastor about her troubles. They seemed to avoid her. She was one lonely woman, with all her emotional and spiritual needs in one basket: her first-ever women's retreat. What a beautiful word. *Retreat.* She needed this retreat at any cost.

She began the 300-mile drive on a blistering Monday morning with high hopes of refreshment, of spiritual renewal, of finding new friends, maybe someone she could open up to, someone who would listen, care, love her.

On the way, over a dollar and a half lunch, Mildred gazed at the brochure, rehearsing the many credits of the speaker. Beautiful, talented, widely published, a pastor's wife. How wonderful to have it all together.

When Mildred arrived at the conference center at 3:00 that afternoon, she was soaked with perspiration. Shy in a new setting, she lugged her belongings to the registration desk. The rooms wouldn't be ready for a couple of hours, and dinner was three hours hence.

Then, the break of a lifetime! One of the retreat directors was looking for someone with a car willing to pick up the speaker at the airport. Would Mildred? Would she ever!

Exhausted, intimidated, yet thrilled, Mildred located the speaker and helped carry her bags to the car. "And what is your role with the retreat, dear?"

"Just an attendee. They needed someone to pick you up."

"Oh. Be careful of the bag, hon. It's leather."

Mildred loaded the trunk. On the way back, the conversation centered on the speaker, her husband, her books, her schedule, her home, her children. Mildred broached the subject of her own son. "Sounds like an ingrate," the speaker said. "I don't know if I could handle that. Do you know when dinner is?"

126

The setting sun brought little break in the temperature. Everyone sat fanning themselves, waiting for dinner, still two hours off. As soon as she could, the speaker extricated herself from the humble chauffeur and became the center of attention. Mildred tried to join the conversation but was ignored.

She felt plain and simple, unimportant and lonely. Until someone discovered the pop machine. Those who had quarters had enough for only one can each. The registration cash box had been put away. Sticky, miserable, suffocating women offered each other dollar bills for two quarters.

Demand quickly outran supply. Before long, two hundred women were in desperate need of change. When it seemed all had resigned themselves to frustration, Mildred slowly rose and moved toward the machine, fishing a roll of quarters from her purse and deftly breaking it open. The coins' clanking and the can's thumping brought a crowd.

Mildred happily made change and accepted the smiles and thanks, drinking in the attention that was every bit as refreshing as the pop. And there stood the speaker. The superstar. In need.

"Uh, Minnie, was it?"

"Mildred."

"Yes, Mildred. Tell me again the name of that daughter I promised to pray for."

"It was my son."

"Oh, yes. And your church. You're active there, you said?"

Mildred nodded.

"And Mildred, did you have any more change?"

28

UNITED, WE FALL

I have seen a subtle, most insidious television commercial, and it is not sexy, lewd, vulgar, or even alcohol-related.

In fact, it drips with respectability. A handsome, distinguished, middle-aged man is talking by phone from a commercial jet. He's telling his boss, I assume, that the next business trip he's been assigned falls on his wedding anniversary. "So you," he says, in essence, "can tell my wife."

Cut to the business trip where he's in charge, salvaging the project, the grateful workers glad he came. Now he's in an airport talking on a pay phone, telling his boss he's on his way home. "Osaka?!" he says.

Next we see him in Osaka.

Then we hear him telling the boss that it's his son's birthday. "Promise you won't call." Cut to the preoccupied dad gazing at a cake with unlit candles, party decorations all about. A look comes over him when the phone rings. And next we see him somewhere else, leading, controlling, succeeding. A champion.

In the space of sixty seconds, one of our leading airline companies—with the voice of an Academy Award winning actor in the background—has sent us a message.

We will take care of you, they say.

When your job is more important than your wife, we'll be there.

When the crisis in Osaka is more important that getting home, we'll get you there in style.

When the boss's call takes precedence over your little boy's birthday, count on us to make your trip enjoyable.

The message is clear: The top priorities for a man today are his job, his career, his status, his ability, his talent, and where it will take him. This man is someone important, someone crucial. He chooses the right airline because the people of that airline understand all this.

And why shouldn't they? In a few years, they'll be flying his children between his home and his former wife's home.

Somehow, the tasteless commercials are easier to deal with than this. We know it's a myth when we see a couple of dozen sun-drenched yuppies cavort as if a

130

light beer makes their day. We've never seen that many good-looking people in one room at one time in our lives, let alone happy.

And if we've ever seen that many people drinking at the same time, we have an idea how many of them end up smiling at all by the end of the evening. More than likely, you'll find some in the bathroom, some on the floor, and too many behind the wheels of cars.

We can also deal with commercials that glorify sexuality in any context. They are so overt, so brazen, from a young man and woman—without shirt and skirt—dancing like superstars in the middle of a brewery to three foxy ladies singing and dancing with a black-eyed dog.

Those are easy to pass off or turn off. But what do we do with the man who is so indispensable that his family comes second?

Don't we want to be like him?

Wouldn't that be something? To be on call any time of the day or night to be flown somewhere in the world where you and only you can solve the critical problem?

The wife will understand.

The kids are resilient.

And aren't you, in the long run, really doing it for them anyway?

The photography, the color, the acting, the music, the script, the narrator, even the company behind it all lend impact, an air of authority, of *rightness*.

But is it right?

> *He who trusts in his riches will fall,*
> *But the righteous will flourish like the*
>   *green leaf.*
> *He who troubles his own house will*
>   *inherit the wind.*
>   *Proverbs 11:28-29, NASB**

---

* *New American Standard Bible.*

29

OF SCANDALS
AND HEDGES

S omeone asked why I had never devoted a column
to the [Jim Bakker] Scandal. I wish I could have
said that enough had written about enough,
but the fact is, were it not for how far in advance one
has to write for a column such as mine, I'd have likely
been on the bandwagon.

But that time has also let me see what everyone
else has said on the subject, so perhaps you deserve a

break today. If there's a debt of gratitude we owe Gary Hart, it's that he—at least briefly—took the spotlight off Jim and Tammy Bakker.

So rather than rehash the pain or pontificate with 20-20 hindsight, maybe there's value in reviewing the hedges we Christians must build around our marriages. I have a list of rather prudish rules that make me look old-fashioned and that I used to be embarrassed to speak of—except to my wife, to whom they are a gift of love.

They are intended to protect my eyes, my heart, my hands, and therefore my marriage. I direct the rules toward appearances and find that if you take care of how things look, you take care of how they are. In other words, if you are never alone with an unrelated female because it might not look appropriate, you have eliminated the possibility that anything inappropriate will take place.

I say these rules will appear prudish because my mentioning them when necessary has elicited squints, scowls, and not-so-hidden smiles of condescension. And in outlining them here, I risk implying that without following my list, I would immediately be plunged into all manner of affairs.

I don't believe that. And in enforcing my own rules I don't mean to insult the many virtuous women who might otherwise have very legitimate reasons to meet or dine with me without the slightest temptation to have designs on me.

Simply hedges, that's all these rules are. And much as people don't like to hear, read, or talk about it, the fact is that most Christian men do not have victory over lust. I have a theory about that. Scripture does not imply that we ever shall have victory over lust the way we are expected to win over worry or greed or malice. Rather, Paul instructs Timothy, and thus us, not to conquer or stand or fight or pray about or resolve, but to *flee* lust.

I know he specifies *youthful* lust, but I don't believe he is limiting it to a certain age, but rather is describing it, regardless at what age it occurs. The little boy in me, and I have room for several, will have to flee lust until I flee life.

Here then are the hedges I build around myself to protect me, my wife, my family, my employer, my church, and, supremely, the reputation of Christ:

1. Whenever I need to meet or dine or travel with an unrelated woman, I make it a threesome. Should an unavoidable last-minute complication make this impossible, my wife hears it from me first.

2. I am careful about touching. Although I might shake hands or squeeze an arm or shoulder in greeting, I embrace only dear friends or relatives, and only in front of others.

3. If I pay a compliment, it is on clothes or hairstyles, not on the person herself. Commenting on a pretty outfit is much different, in my opinion, than telling a woman that she herself looks pretty.

4. I avoid flirtation or suggestive conversation, even in jest.

5. I remind my wife often in writing and orally that I remember my wedding vows: "Keeping you only unto me for as long as we both shall live. . . ." Dianna is not the jealous type, nor has she ever demanded such assurances from me. She does, however, appreciate my rules and my observances of them.

6. From the time I get home from work until the children go to bed, I do no writing or office work. This gives me lots of time with the family and for my wife and me to continue to court and date.

I share this not to boast but to admit that I'm still fleeing, and in the hope that there be some benefit to someone.

30

FIRST CLASS GRACE

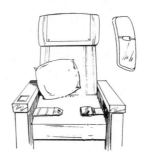

Wouldn't call it an epiphany, but maybe a small, not wholly adequate glimpse of grace. You stumble onto such things in unlikely places. For me it was at Washington's National Airport. This was one of those up-at-5:00 A.M. and home-by-10:00 P.M. jobs. On top of that, the assignment had been unpleasant.

I was tired and must have looked it when I finally showed up at the gate so they'd know that one more pre-reserved, non-smoking aisle to Chicago had checked in. All the man at the desk had to do was stamp my boarding pass, but he said something strange.

"It's Friday night, and I'm goin' home after this flight."

"Me too," I joked. But he wasn't listening.

"Let's see if we can find you a better seat, and I'll buy you a drink." He said all this while tapping at the keyboard and stamping a new seat assignment and pass.

Passengers were boarding. He wasn't inviting me to join him for a nightcap. I knew what he meant. His work week was almost over, and I looked like someone who could use a first-class seat at no extra charge—and a free drink.

He thought I'd appreciate both, and I could tell from the look on his face that it made him feel good. I didn't tell him the free drink was wasted on me. I just thanked him.

And when I boarded, I was struck by the similarities between Christians and first-class passengers:

We were set apart.

We were there because our names were on a list.

We were treated like royalty.

We had privileges that others did not.

There were also major differences, of course, because no illustration holds up entirely:

Most had paid for the privilege. For all I knew, I was the only one there on a free pass.

The man who showed the grace was giving me something that cost him nothing. In fact, it wasn't really his to give.

Being saved from coach class is a far cry from being saved from hell.

I sat there not wanting anyone in first class or coach to know that I didn't belong.

138

Maybe if there had been an easy way for many others to enjoy the same privilege, I would have shared the good news. "Yes, go see the man at the ticket counter. He'll give you a new seat assignment, free! Just ask! He *wants* to do it!"

Or would I have? Perhaps there are more similarities to my first-class gift and my gift of salvation than I'm comfortable to admit. Maybe I'd rather just enjoy the ride than see that others enjoy it, too.

Maybe I'd rather pretend that somehow I deserved it, that I belong in God's first-class family, that I'm not here because a friendly Agent put my name on the list.

31

BUNNY WEEK,
INDEED

Y ou've got to hand it to Jews for Jesus. It takes
guts to be one, and they are overt in the nicest
ways possible.

The ministry's very name offends many Jews, and
yet, what is better than being honest? No trickery. No
deception. You can't even say that about certain home
buying services or some evangelistic ministries.

Sure they stand on street corners and hand out literature, but no one is obstructed, no one is horse-collared, no one is shouted at or preached at or even touched. They boldly wear T-shirts announcing that they are Jews for Jesus. If that offends you, you can walk by.

Staff members of Jews for Jesus are Jews *for* Jesus, and they make that clear. They're currently being attacked and lumped with cultic and other groups who are obnoxious in public places and spoil it for the good guys.

Anyone who has traveled has been victimized by the others. You're innocently working your way through a major airport when someone accosts you by pinning something on you or handing you a book, and you find yourself awkwardly engaged in a conversation.

Recently a young woman sat next to me as I waited for a plane. "Have you heard the news?" she asked. I shook my head, returning her smile, hoping she would be a Christian who might be encouraged to discover another one.

"It's national bunny week," she said, quickly clipping three furry little bunnies to my sleeve. You can imagine how a (very) grown man feels sitting in an airport with bunnies hanging from his arm.

I prayed she wasn't with *Playboy*. She wasn't. She said she worked with emotionally disturbed young people (forgive me, but I confess I wondered how recently she had graduated from the program). I could contribute to the program by buying one bunny for $5 or two for $9.

Then, I suppose, I would qualify for the program.

I declined. She asked if I wanted to just donate a dollar. I didn't. I have no quarrel with her work, but her approach was all wrong. Believe me, it's not hard to say no when you'd give just about anything to get those bunnies off your arm.

Her smile disappeared, and she quickly removed

her bunnies. I was relieved. I felt a little cheap and a little guilty, which is all part of the deal, I guess. Until I heard the reaction she got from a young mother across the way.

"Are you kidding? I don't even know you or what you want, and you pin bunnies on me? Forget it!"

I saw the girl half an hour later sans bunnies, with a fistful of fives. Just because it works doesn't mean it's right.

Jews for Jesus doesn't believe in embarrassing people. You'll never find yourself an unwilling captive audience. If you want to talk or listen, you'll know in advance who they are and what they're up to.

They believe in Jesus and take seriously the Great Commission. They believe that Los Angeles International Airport, among other public places, is an appropriate venue for exercising their First Amendment rights, as long as they don't harass, embarrass, detain, or solicit.

Pray for them as the U.S. Supreme Court deliberates. . . .

[They won.]

32

STOP
ON A DIME

Allentown, Pennsylvania, has an efficient little airport that's as pleasant as any if you have to sit and wait. I was on my way home, and I missed my kids.

I often say it that way—that I miss my kids, without including the fact that I miss their mother, my wife, too. Dianna knows that missing her goes without saying.

We're one. And when I am away and miss the kids, she feels for me, even though she might rather be with me and enjoy the chance to miss them a little.

One of the reasons I missed my boys was that I had just spent a couple of days in the home of Ron and Christine Wyrtzen. The popular Christian recording artist and her husband have an adopted daughter and son, and the very close and special relationship they all have can make you long for home.

Ron and Christine talk to their kids. They listen to them. They include them, care about them, treat them like equals. They don't pretend the kids don't need supervision, guidance, and discipline, but in the Wyrtzen home, children are people.

That environment stood in clear contrast to what happened at the Allentown airport on my way out of town. I sat near a mother and her four- or five-year-old daughter. Standing near us in the busy gate area was a middle-aged couple in animated conversation. As they chatted, the man pulled his hands from his pockets to gesture and a dime slipped out and bounced to the floor, rolling near his feet.

Neither the man nor his wife noticed. But the little girl and her mother did. The girl made a move for the dime, but the mother grabbed her arm. "I want that dime, Mommy," the girl whispered.

What an opportunity to teach a child ethics, fairness, politeness, courtesy!

"I know," her mother said, giggling. "Wait till they walk away."

"He doesn't see it!" the girl said.

"I know. Just wait." The girl fought against her mother's grip. "Just wait, honey," she said. "As soon as he leaves, you can have it."

The man and his wife looked toward the ticket counter. The mother and daughter tensed, smiling. When the couple began to move, I picked up the dime. "Excuse me, sir. You dropped this."

The man looked incredulous. "Hey, thanks a lot."

As I sat back down, I stole a glance at the mother and child. I wasn't trying to be self-righteous or smug. A dime might seen insignificant, but I grieved for that child and the values she was learning. I could only hope her saucer-eyed look indicated that she wished she had given the dime back to the man.

There was no question about the young mother's tight-lipped scowl. She wished I'd minded my own business. I wished her daughter *was* my business. And despite what I tried to say with a stern return of her gaze, I'm still kicking myself for not saying anything.

Like: "Great job of parenting, lady. I hope your daughter doesn't grow up to be a certified public accountant. Or a civic leader. Or a mother like you."

Mercy. It's better I kept my mouth shut.

33

Some Call It the Ghetto

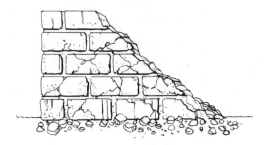

I'm brimming with sensory overload. My job was to not only learn about a wholistic ministry in the heart of Chicago's West Side ghetto, but to also experience it. I took my wife, Dianna, so that I would also benefit from her unique perspective. (Tiny black children were drawn to her like magnets, climbing into her lap without hesitation.)

Circle Urban Ministries reaches the predominantly black community known as the Austin District. Circle is run by Glen Kehrein, who is white, and with whom I attended Moody Bible Institute more than twenty years ago. I can't say I knew him then, but after spending a couple of days with him, I wish I could say otherwise.

Glen is the archetypical activist, a man so committed to and wrapped up in other people's needs that he is not even aware of his own selflessness and sacrifice.

He does not dwell on himself. He saw a need twenty years ago, prepared himself to help meet it, and has stayed at the task in spite of disappointments and hardships. His primary commitment is to Christ, and against all odds and prevailing "wisdom," he has given himself to cross-cultural, interracial ministry.

Circle Urban feeds the hungry, clothes the poor, counsels the needy, houses the homeless, advises the oppressed, and seeks to effect justice for the downtrodden. But above all, it presents the saving claims of Christ.

The ministry is housed in a block-long former school building, and it works hand-in-hand with The Rock of Our Salvation Evangelical Free Church, pastored by Raleigh Washington (a black), which operates out of the same facility.

Eat breakfast before attending 9:30 A.M. Sunday school and 11:00 A.M. Sunday service. Otherwise, you'll get light-headed from hunger by the early afternoon when the stirring singing, rousing preaching, praying, and testifying have ended. It's an exciting place to go to church, and the sermons are rich and deep.

Twenty percent of the congregation is white, and several join the choir for traditional black singing. The congregation joins hands at the end for a unique doxology. These people love and respect each other. They work together. They don't make a big deal out of it. They just do it. See the need? Join us. Hung up on the interracial thing? Stay in suburbia.

The church was suffering that Sunday because the

evil of the neighborhood had invaded the congregation—its lives, its souls. During the week, a six-year-old
boy, a Sunday schooler at The Rock, had been killed by
a stray bullet while sitting on his back porch.

During the service, in broad daylight on a busy
street, a parishioner's car parked in front of the church
was broken into and relieved of its radio. During the
evening service, pastor Washington thundered:

"The cowards who broke into our sister's car will
not drive us from our community! The murderers
whose stray bullet took the life of one of our precious
children will not drive us from our neighborhood!
Some call it the ghetto; I call it home!"

Pastor Washington came to Christ as an adult, a
career army lieutenant colonel. Five years later, Trinity
Seminary-trained, he felt called to preach Christ in one
of the highest crime-rate neighborhoods anywhere. The
new church needed a wholistic ministry. The existing
wholistic ministry needed a church anchor.

Could the white Kehrein and the black Washington
make it work? They hit it off. Became friends. They are
forthright and honest with one another.

It's working.

34

LOVE ON A WINTER'S NIGHT

When Dianna and I began having children, I knew I would one day get a glimpse of God's unconditional father love. I enjoyed reading of parents overcome by emotion, willing to do anything for their children.

Parents understand God's sorrow over broken relationships. They understand what it means to hate the sin and love the sinner. They know what it means to love someone no matter what. They learn what their parents endured, and they realize they may have been wrong in assuming they couldn't tell their parents everything.

I'd like to think my boys can tell me anything. Nothing they say or do could lessen my love for them. They're fourteen, twelve, and seven now, and I have a good relationship with each. I believe they're confident of my love for them, though I can't presume they tell me *everything*. I want them always to feel free to talk to me about any problem, and if memory serves, our oldest is already more frank with me than I was with my parents.

I don't know what I was afraid of, but now that I'm a parent, I know I couldn't have shocked or disappointed my parents to the point where they would have disowned me. (Right, Mom?)

Parenting, with all its ups and downs and frustrations and fears, remains the most fun part of my life. Other pleasures give temporary rushes, but what can provide as deep a sense of satisfaction as knowing your child has received Christ, has learned to be kind, to think of others first, to work before he plays?

What could be more gratifying than to hear a child say, unsolicited and unprompted, "Love you, Dad"?

Our youngest, Michael, is currently the most cuddly. He's a lanky firstgrader who still has a baby face. He never lets me get out the door without a "Hug/kiss! Hug/kiss!" He's also still excited when I pull into the driveway in the afternoon, running to jump into my arms.

It was Michael who prompted my latest rush of emotional love. I had put him to bed an hour before. Dianna was at a meeting, and Dallas and Chad were at piano lessons in town, ten minutes away. Dianna and I discussed the possibility that Michael would be asleep when it came time for me to drive in and pick up the other two.

Should I just let him sleep, assuming he wouldn't stir during my twenty-minute absence? What could happen? We came to no conclusion before Dianna left, so when the time came for the run into town, the decision was mine.

The downside of taking him with me was that I would interrupt his deep, sound sleep, which any child needs. The four of us would just barely fit in my small car for the ride back. A prowler? A fire? A water problem?

You can imagine how brief was the mental debate. I crept into Michael's room, gathered his quilt about him, and lugged him out into the wintry night. Dead to the world, he wrapped his arms around my neck and breathed heavily in my ear.

I could have held him like that forever, but I had to set him down to shut the back door. I scooped him up and deposited him in the car, where he immediately stretched out in the back seat.

Halfway into town, I heard him stir. He raised his head.

"What's my blanket doin' in here?"

"You're sleeping, Michael. We're going to pick up the boys."

When we got there, he sat up to make room. The older two chattered about their lessons, and Michael laid his head in Chad's lap. They didn't notice that I wasn't upholding my end of the conversation. I was overwhelmed with love for my boys and moved by the thought that my heavenly Father loves me even more than that (Matthew 7:11).

35

ANGUISH
IN THE NIGHT

When Raymond was awakened by the phone after midnight one Saturday morning, his wife didn't stir. As he made his way to the living room, his thoughts raced to his two married sons and a daughter in college.

He hoped for a wrong number. Phone calls in the night rarely bring good news. He offered a sleepy, muffled, octave-lower-than-usual, "Hello?"

All he heard was sobbing. he prayed silently, "Father, give me strength for whatever is wrong."

"Daddy?" the female voice managed.

"Yes," Raymond answered, his voice thick from sleep. His daughter just sobbed. Raymond whispered so as not to disturb his wife, "Honey, what is it?"

"Oh, Daddy!" she said, fighting for control. He waited. "Daddy, I'm sorry."

Raymond hoped it was only a failed test, a failed class, a failed semester. She cried and cried. "Daddy?" she said.

"I'm here," he said.

"Daddy, I'm pregnant."

Raymond's heart sank. How could it be? He and his wife had raised their children in love, in the church, from the Bible. Each member of the family had a personal relationship with Christ, and each had an unusual ability to interact with the others. The kids had always been open about their struggles and temptations.

Yet Raymond didn't even know that his daughter had a boyfriend. Was the father a new love? Had she been forced? Was it someone he knew? With the phone pressed to his ear, his free hand covering his eyes, he prayed silently for strength, for the right words, the right response. He was broken-hearted.

Raymond had always feared he might explode in anger and embarrassment over such news. Yet now he found himself overcome with sympathy, pity, protectiveness for his precious child, still in the bloom of youth.

His daughter—clearly distressed, broken, repentant—begged for forgiveness. Raymond didn't ask for details. "We love you," he said through his tears. "We forgive you."

He was on the phone more than a half-hour, then sat crying until dawn when his wife padded out to hear the news. They went through the day in their pajamas, hardly eating, working on a letter. It assured their daughter that they would always be there for her and the baby, and that they would be available to cousel her or to support her decision on what to do about the father.

The post office promised the letter would be delivered early Monday morning. The waiting was torture.

Raymond prayed all weekend that God would somehow erase history, would put things back the way they had been just a few hours before.

On Monday morning a pale, bleary-eyed Raymond went to work. Midmorning he took a call from his daughter. "Daddy," she said, laughing, "what in the world is this letter all about?"

It had not been a joke. Not a crank call. It had been a wrong number—a tragic mistake in the middle of the night—two people in turmoil thinking they knew to whom they were talking. Raymond spent the rest of the day vainly trying to help the phone company determine *where* the call could have originated. He didn't want a girl racing home to a father she thought had forgiven her, only to find that he knew nothing about her situation.

Raymond, an old acquaintance, is a saint. He admits it was the most traumatic experience he's ever had, but he is grateful that it has made him sensitive to parents who do receive such unbearable news. "For forty-eight hours, my wife and I ached."

In a way, though, God answered Raymond's prayer. With the Monday call, everything had been put back the way it had been. Everything except Raymond. He will never be the same.

36

A DAD BY
ANY OTHER NAME

S he calls me Honey and I call her Babe, but when she or the boys talk about me, they all call me Dad. Dianna wouldn't say, "Go ask Honey to come upstairs," or, "Go ask my husband." She doesn't even call me "your dad," as many mothers refer to their husbands.

I'm just Dad. It's my favorite name. Oh, it's embarrassing when Dianna forgets that my lunch bag doesn't have to be differentiated from thirty others—like the kids' lunches do—and writes DAD on it in big, block letters. But I still like the name.

I'm Dad to my fourteen-year-old. Someday I'll be Dad to all of them, and I'll miss the Daddy part. When I once shaved off my beard, Michael said, "Now you look like the *real* Daddy!"

I'm still young enough to be uncomfortable being called Mister. When I hear "Mr. Jenkins," I look for my own dad. Though being called Dad reminds me that I can remember Dad when he was my age, I have to let it sink in that I play the same role with my boys that he played with his.

He was, and is, everything to us. It didn't impact my brothers and me that he was raised without a father, until we were grown and had children of our own. We can't imagine having grown up without a father. And I'm sure my brothers wonder, as I do, at what a father he was and is, considering he had no model.

Our family has a strange custom. Though we are all relatively outgoing and social-minded, when we get together—even after having not seen each other for months—we seem to take each other in stride.

The lack of enthusiasm in our greetings doesn't mean anything. It surprises people who expect us to embrace or exult, but that's just something we've never done. Yet feelings run deep. I sense as much affection in our casually picking up conversations—and relationships—where they left off as I would in a joyous reception.

Part of that, of course, comes from Dad. He's a humorous man and an articulate poet, but not overly expressive. "Still waters run deep" and "strong, silent type" are the cliches. A man's man, a Marine, a police chief, still he is always polite, soft-spoken, considerate, a gentleman.

162

He doesn't consider it old-fashioned to open a door for a woman or to rise when she enters the room. He's been told he's "honest to a fault"—quite a commentary if you think about it.

Best of all, he's been a one-woman man all his life. If it's true that the best thing a father can do for his children is to love their mother, my brothers and I had the best thing done for us from the days we were born. Dad is an unabashed romantic and proves his love every day.

He was a model in his willingness to scrub floors, change diapers, cook, or do whatever else needed doing when all four boys were home and Mom needed help. He was never too much man for that. He didn't just tell us what to do.

It's said we get our first and most lasting image of God from our fathers. That makes me grateful. Grateful that my dad is not an alcoholic. Grateful that he is faithful. Grateful that he is industrious. Grateful that he loved his sons unconditionally and proved it more than once.

I'm grateful Dad's priorities are right and uncompromising. Grateful that he cares more about people than things, more about family than money, more about loyalty and integrity than image.

He's not perfect like the heavenly Father. But to have half his character is my loftiest dream. To be thought of one day the way my brothers and I think of our dad. . . .

The only thing he didn't teach me was how to comfortably tell him out loud that I love him. But I do, Dad.

37

BEST FRIENDS

I have a best friend. I'm not talking about my wife, who is more than a best friend. I'm talking about a guy my age whom I have known since the first week of college.

His name is Dave. He is a pastor. We see each other twice, maybe three times a year. With him I can truly be myself. It isn't that I am deceptive with all others, but we do tend to put our best foot forward when relationships are at risk, don't we?

Having to be on our best behavior most of the time isn't all bad. But at times I need to let my hair down, tell somebody *everything*, revert to adolescence, and enjoy a relationship built on years of trust and confidence.

Where else—outside my family—can I sing aloud to oldies on the radio, laugh till I cry, recall childish pranks with humor rather than embarrassment, and be myself, warts and all? Dave and I tease that we each have enough knowledge to ruin the other's reputation.

Our schedules don't allow our families (he and his wife have four children, we have three) to vacation together this summer at a Bible conference center, as we've done for years. I'll miss it. His Diane and my Dianna wonder how relaxed and refreshed we can be after spending all day with the kids, all evening with our wives, and the rest of the night talking and playing games while our families sleep.

We wonder the same, but somehow it works. It's what we need. Ours is a friendship that endures, that picks up where it leaves off, even after months of no contact. For some reason, busyness I suppose, we hardly ever write or call. We simply live in our own orbits, then debrief each other when the families get together.

It amazes me how similar are our struggles and victories. Our gifts are not similar. His are in organization, people relations, and teaching. Our backgrounds are both different and similar: Dave grew up with sisters, I with brothers, but we were both raised by devout, active evangelicals, quiet, behind-the-scenes type people.

We met the first week at college, hit it off, and talked all night. We've drifted from the others who ran in our crowd more than twenty years ago, but Dave and I are bonded by someone he introduced me to. His girl friend, Diane, knew a girl she and Dave thought I should meet. We've been married more than eighteen years. Dave and I were in each other's weddings.

Though separated by a couple hundred miles, Dave and I have been "together" through job changes, moves, disappointments, heartaches, and joys. This fall (1989) we'll each turn forty. I've been gray for fifteen years. He recently started shaving.

When I think of Dave, I'm often reminded of a conversation I had with the crusty, old publisher of the first newspaper I worked for. He once mentioned that he had a twenty-five-year friendship. He must have noticed my blank expression. At barely nineteen I didn't understand the significance. "How many people do you know," he asked, "who have the same friend for that long? Someone who's not related?"

He had a point.

"Someday," he added, "you'll realize how rare it is to have a friend for that long."

Dave's and my friendship is pushing twenty-two years. We've seen each other's children grow from infancy to adolescence. I am beginning to see the wisdom of the old publisher's comment.

I have other good friends, at least two of whom I consider particularly close. But Dave and I have stood the test of time. We'll make twenty-five years, if God chooses, and it wouldn't surprise me if we were friends as grandparents one day.

I only wish our families could have vacationed this summer as usual. Next year, Dave.

38

HAPPY
NEW YEAR

I know, I know. It's September. But as one who
loves new beginnings, starting over, and clean
slates, for me September is as wonderful as
January.

Lots of things start in September. School starts.
Fall starts. Football starts.

I was born in September. The only problem with my birthday this year [1989] is that it's the big four-oh. I don't expect it to be traumatic, but I do worry a little about several friends who beat me to that birthday and who have accurate memories of my celebrations for them.

Actually, I don't think this birthday will be any different. I don't dread it. It's another new beginning, a chance to reflect on grace and on blessing no one deserves, a chance to look ahead to what should be a productive and fun season of life.

My youngest son, Michael, was also born in September. He'll turn seven three weeks before I turn forty, and he keeps me young. I'm still required to chase him upstairs every night so he can dive into his bed ahead of me.

After I was interviewed on local television last summer, he greeted me with, "Dad, I saw you on TV! You shoulda been here!" Recently, when we were in unfamiliar territory in the car, he said, "Dad, are you a man who knows where he's going?"

We laughed. He didn't know he was being profound. Yet his was a question for the ages.

39

FOREVER FRIENDS

The early 1970s saw Barb Goodwin and Jill Wilson move from downstate Illinois to Chicago to seek their fortunes. Barb found work in a music shop, Jill in a book shop. Times were turbulent, confusing. The young women had been best-friend children of the '60s. They were searching, for what they did not know.

They experimented, listened, discussed, read, ran with various crowds. One day Barb bought Jill a gift. It was innocuous, Barb thought. Just something to read and think about—a book on Transcendental Meditation.

But from the day she gave it to Jill, late in 1975, Barb felt guilty. Why? They were open-minded. What could be wrong with looking into TM?

Barb didn't know. All she knew was that she felt terrible about the gift and was compelled to replace it. One lunch hour she visited the Moody Bookstore in the Loop, where she discovered *The Living Bible*. Here was a book every bit as valid for a couple of searching young women, and Barb knew she would feel better about giving it to Jill.

For several days Barb tried to muster the courage to ask Jill for the TM book. When she finally stammered her request to replace the original gift, Jill was stunned nearly to silence. A month later, however, she too had begun to visit Moody's Loop store.

When Jill discovered *How to Be a Christian in an Unchristian World*, by Fritz Ridenour, she devoured it. Its simple presentation of the gospel made sense. She believed for the first time that God was the Creator, that Jesus was His Son who had died for her sins. In November 1975, she prayed and received Christ as her Savior.

Suddenly she couldn't get enough of her *Living Bible*. Barb was almost jealous, and when Jill wasn't reading the volume, Barb was. In January 1976, Barb, too, came to faith in Christ. She remembers the next month as almost comical. The roommates competed for time with the Bible, often reading well into the night. They attended Moody Church, listened to Moody radio, and attended every session of Moody Founder's Week in February.

They were flush with their first love of Christ, eager to devote their lives to Him. They applied for work at Moody Bible Institute, and Jill enrolled in the

Advanced Studies Program. She eventually became manager of the Moody Bookstore in the Loop; Barb became film rental manager and later retail director in charge of all Moody bookstores. Jill transferred to an editorial position in Moody Press and then, in March 1988, to *Moody Monthly.*

Over the years, Barb and Jill became beloved favorites of their co-workers. Barb is quiet, almost shy, a respected retail and management expert. In private she can be wry and hilarious. Jill was a wordsmith, a trivia buff, a loyal friend. She also served Christ in private, anonymous ways. Few friends knew she had "adopted" a little sister from the nearby housing projects.

One recent fateful weekend, tragedy visited Barb and Jill. An auto accident took Jill's life and that of Barb's mother and left Barb in the hospital with multiple fractures.

Jill was a week older than I. We joked that I had to respect her as my elder and that she planned to stall at thirty-nine and let me reach forty before her. I'll always wish she hadn't been unintentionally prophetic.

Barb and Jill's many friends neither understand nor like what has happened, but we accept the responsibility to take God's sovereignty at face value and to prove His love to Barb and her family and to Jill's family.

Barb is consoled only by what she calls "the privilege of having known Jill before and after Christ." And though we who knew and loved Jill have suffered a deep loss, we too are comforted by the knowledge that Christian friends like Jill are friends forever.

40

PARENTING 101

Baseball season becomes football season, and that
turns into basketball and soccer seasons. Before
you know it, spring baseball will be here again.
If you're a parent, the whole year is one big carpool
season.

We complain about it, but in truth Dianna and I
love it. Once we've figured out who goes where and

when and who will watch which kid, we settle into our lawn chairs and enjoy.

Usually I meet the family at the game on my way home from work. Dianna brings healthy munchies to tide us over. It's all great fun and I'll never forget it, even if the kids do. Which I doubt they will.

Seven years separate our eldest and youngest of three boys, and Dallas, fourteen, has already pledged that, like his dad, he will always make it to as many of Michael's games as possible. "He's had to sit through all of mine," Dal explains.

It's heartwarming to see brothers support and encourage one another. I suppose it's helped that Dallas has had his sport (basketball), Chad his (baseball), and Michael his (soccer, so far). But they really are proud of one another. Attending one of our kids' games is one of the funnest things we do together.

Win or lose, we're all in it together. It's a priority. It's also a lesson for all of us. In nearly every game we see examples of good sportsmanship and bad sportsmanship. We see coaches (fortunately usually only opposing coaches) who care more about winning than about having fun or developing character or teaching fundamentals.

We see good players who are lazy and bad players who hustle. We see the occasional good player who hustles, which makes him great. We see (and hear) fans who know how to encourage and cheer and be good sports, and we see (and hear) the opposite.

Our favorite bad example of a parent/coach was in charge of a visiting team. Apparently he had been a great baseball player in his day. He was embarrassed by the performance of his players, and he said so, loud and often and from all over the field.

He carried on a play-by-play harangue of every missed opportunity, every taken strike, every bad throw or missed ball. Admittedly, there were many. His team was inept. But they were young and eager. That eagerness died as the game wore on.

They fell further and further behind, and their spirits were broken by the endless badgering for all to hear. The players made blunder after blunder, their eyes cast down, their shoulders stooped. And the coach continued, "That's no way to throw! I'm embarrassed! If you can't do any better than that, you might as well sit down! I've never seen anything like this in my life!"

But then, a miracle of miracles. With the bases loaded, several runs already in, and two outs, one of our hitters drove a sky-high pop-up toward second base. The shortstop on the ill-fated team circled beneath it, fear on his face.

At the last instant he stabbed at the ball and it stuck in his glove. His teammates cheered. Even our fans applauded. He looked expectantly at his coach. Surely this would earn some morsel of praise.

"If you'd missed that one, you'd have run forty laps tomorrow!" the coach said.

What a sad picture. If it's true that our views of God come from our parents and others in authority over us, imagine what those players think of Him.

In life we're all players on a bad team. We try. We fail. We mess up. We sin. But our eyes don't have to be cast down, our shoulders don't have to be stooped. Our Coach takes us as we are and makes us into something better. And what do we hear?

"Well done, good and faithful servant."

We parents and coaches can take a lesson.

41

OUT OF
AFRICA

NAIROBI, KENYA, EAST AFRICA—I love the smells here. When you step out into the crisp, equatorial mountain air each morning, sunny or cloudy, there is the aroma of roasting breakfasts.

Somehow the burning fat, the vegetables being steamed for lunch, and the maize roasted over coals in the open air overcomes the stench of canal water, public garbage dumps, and the belching of black diesel exhaust from cars, trucks, and overcrowded buses.

Most of the houses are close, even connected, and each tiny drive and yard is protected by stone walls and padlocked iron gates. Yet children frolic in the streets, dashing out of the way of compact cars barreling up the left side. My six-year-old is an instant hit with the wee black faces who clamor for the right to play with his G.I. Joes.

"Michael! Michael!" they cry every morning. He dashes out with "Hey, dudes!" and they giggle and wrestle and fight over Joes and paddles and balls and Frisbees. The little sweat-suited emissary has never been so popular. He won't realize until later that his toys bought this attention. For now he enjoys his new friends, friends who gleefully call him "White Bread."

I'm here for a couple of weeks to teach writing and editing at Daystar University College in this capital city of one of Africa's most lush and beautiful countries. You think Africa, and you imagine blazing heat and thatched-roof huts.

But it's winter here in the big city. While there is crippling poverty, there is also hot water, indoor plumbing, showers, paved roads, traffic jams. You'll also see a herd of small goats prodded up the side streets. People without cars walk on well-worn dirt paths that crisscross the area.

I catch a ride with a professor in the mornings and make the twenty-minute walk home in the evenings. Our place is strange and different, but it quickly became comfortable. We miss our real home, but none of the five of us would want to be here without the others. And it's only for less than three weeks.

The short time you're here, you stick to bottled water, and you eat out at hotels or nice restaurants as often as your schedule and budget allow. And you're impressed with people, blacks and whites, Americans, Canadians, British, and Africans.

They look and sound different here, but they are the same as everywhere. They have dreams and goals, families, careers, ministries. More than two hundred students jam a minuscule campus in town, most sponsored by friends, families, churches, or mission agencies.

In my magazine editing class I asked the students if they could use an extra day past the original due date for the first draft of the articles. Not only did they not want an extra day, but they also wanted to turn in their manuscripts a day early. Every student.

And on a quiz, which I purposely made very specific and detailed because the students had done so swimmingly on the first one, a student astounded me. I gave the class a few minutes to review their notes, feeling remorse in advance for the complexity of the test, but Mr. Mbutu had not brought his notes with him.

He did not look on with anyone else, and he said he had not reviewed his notes in advance either. I know he didn't cheat because he sat in the front row, a few feet from me, during the quiz. Yet he not only got a perfect score, but also, on an extra-credit question where I maddeningly asked for a regurgitation of a list of six things we discussed, he enumerated them all and in the order they had been covered.

There is a discernible desperation here to learn, develop, and get into ministry. My family and I will be glad to get home, but we'll never forget the sights and sounds and smells, and especially the people. The game parks and the animals are magnificent, but it's the spirit and joy and dedication of the people that made the trip worth everything.

42

COME AS A CHILD

She would turn five in three scant weeks, and she knew her mind. It was a Sunday night, just before bedtime, and Lynnette Gauger chose just the book she wanted Daddy to read.

It wasn't the first time Jon Gauger had read *My Friend Jesus*, by Ella Lindvall (Moody Press). Lynnette loved the sounds of the words and the stories from the

Bible; Jon appreciated the carefully designed kid-orientation. "It delightfully presents the plan of salvation and gently asks questions that require thought and action."

When the book was finished, it was hugs and kisses all around and the customary night-night squeeze. Twenty minutes later Lynnette padded out to the living room in tears. "I was thinking about Great Grandma and how she is in heaven."

Jon and his wife looked at each other. Lynnette had always been an emotional girl, especially when she was tired. Her great-grandmother had died a year and half before, and Lynnette still felt the loss.

"I know someday we'll see her again," she continued, "but thinking about her made me sad, so I started singing a song about Jesus. Then I decided to ask Him into my heart."

Whoops! Warning lights and bells went off in Jon's head. This was an event he and his wife had prayed for, but could Lynnette really understand, at four years old?

"Would you like to pray with Mom and Dad?" he asked, still wondering. She nodded.

Jon recalls wanting to ask her "five thousand questions, not to discourage her, but to determine whether she really understood." He limited himself to just a few, in her language.

"What does it mean to ask Jesus into your heart?"

"It means to believe He died on the cross for our sins."

"What is sin?"

"Doing bad things."

"Do you ever sin?"

"Yes."

"What does it mean to believe in Jesus?"

"It means we go to heaven when we die."

After a few more questions, the Gaugers felt Lynnette was clear on the concept, and they helped her pray a prayer of acknowledgment of who God is, that she realized she needed His forgiveness, that she believed Jesus died for her sins, and that she wanted to live for Him.

The next night Lynnette asked for the same book, and three days later, in the car with Daddy, she noticed a cloud formation that looked just like one from *My Friend Jesus*. "Is that where Jesus lives?" she asked. "Up there in that cloud?"

"Jesus lives far beyond the highest clouds, Lynnette," Jon said. "It sure is great to think about those things, isn't it?"

She nodded. "Daddy," she said slowly, "when you're a Christian, you wonder about Jesus."

If Jon had had any doubt of the validity of his daughter's experience with Christ, it was gone now. He asked himself, *How much do I wonder about Jesus? How much wonder do I have for my own salvation?*

There will be those who will question Lynnette's salvation experience. They will point to her fear of death, her longing to be with Great Grandma, and a book or parent who might have unintentionally manipulated her with the best intentions.

But you won't get any of that from this corner. I received Christ at six, as did one of my sons. The other two were four. When they are teens and have faint recollections of their childhood decisions, Lynnette and my boys will likely rededicate themselves to a faith they want to be sure was not inherited. But nobody will convince me they haven't already put their faith in Christ.

"Assuredly, I say to you, whoever does not receive the kingdom of God as a little child will by no means enter it" (Luke 18:17, NKJV*).

* *New King James Version.*